THE FEARLESS REVOLUTIONARY

THE FEARLESS REVOLUTIONARY

The True Account Of ***Kanaklata Barua's*** Sacrifice for India's Freedom

HIRANYA BORAH

An imprint of
Srishti Publishers & Distributors

Srishti Publishers & Distributors
A unit of AJR Publishing LLP
212A, Peacock Lane
Shahpur Jat, New Delhi – 110 049

editorial@srishtipublishers.com

First published in India by
Blue Rose Publishers in 2023

First Published by Bold,
an imprint of Srishti Publishers & Distributors in 2024

Copyright © Hiranya Borah, 2024

10 9 8 7 6 5 4 3 2 1

This is a work of non-fiction based on the author's research about the subject and interviews with their next of kin, friends and associates. While due care has been taken by the author and publisher to verify contents at press time, any inadvertent miss that is brought to their notice shall be duly verified and updated subsequently. Actual names of people and places have been used with a view to provide first-hand information.

The author asserts the moral right to be identified as the author of this work.

All rights reserved. No part of this publication may be reproduced, stored in a retrieval system, or transmitted, in any form or by any means, electronic, mechanical, photocopying, recording or otherwise, without the prior written permission of the Publishers.

Printed and bound in India

The book is dedicated to the lesser-known martyrs, the unsung heroes and heroines of India since time immemorial, who laid down their lives while defending our borders or while driving out illegal occupants. Their numbers may be unimaginably large, but they have not stayed alive in public memory for even a year or two, despite the fact that the general public enjoys political and economic independence due to their supreme sacrifices.

A NOTE FROM THE AUTHOR

This book does not claim a hundred percent authenticity of facts, though I have tried my best to collect all information correctly as far as the historical accounts are concerned. The character of Hari Hara Rajkhowa is a fictitious one, however based on a real person who was injured in the firing incident that took place at Gohpur Police Station on 20th September 1942. In case someone comes forward with authentic documents and reasonable arguments against my views presented in the book, I will be happy to revisit the same.

Preface

On a visit to the Triveni Sangam,
I saw with my naked eyes;
Two of the largest rivers of India
Embrace each other with love and passion.
On the next visit,
I felt,
The sound of music and dance,
Of enticing waves making rooms
In the hearts and minds
Of sages of ancient India.
Me, an ignorant of the twentieth century,
Could not fathom from
Where those sounds of music were coming
Till I felt the heart wrenching cacophony
Of a lost river known as Saraswati.
I saw the Tiranga more than thousand times;
I could not see beyond the three colours
And the moving Chakra
Eulogising the progress of peaceful journey
Of a modern country.
I flipped the pages of life of a martyr yesterday,
I felt the presence of
Thousands of droplets of blood

Soaked in a piece of cloth,
Without red bloody colour
And the smell of fresh blood,
Like Saraswati is flowing
Without any visual delight
And any sweet sound of music.

***

Around two years ago, during one of my visits to Guwahati from Delhi, a highly educated Assamese gentleman requested me to write a book on Kanaklata Barua (I am told that the British Parliament took note of the martyrdom of this young lady at the age of 17 in the police firing that took place at the west gate of Gohpur police station of the erstwhile Darrang District, Assam on 20th September 1942 during the 1942 Quit India movement. It was claimed that she was the first teenaged girl shot dead by the British police in the freedom movement of India. This gentleman wanted me to write a book on her, along with some other unsung heroes and heroines with the aim that they'd become household names in India. I appreciated his concern about the martyrs, but I explained my reservations of writing a full-scale book on her at that time.

The first and foremost was that there was a paucity of authentic documents on her. Secondly, no established publisher would come forward to publish a biography of a lesser-known martyr. If I self-published the biography, I know that the number of readers outside Assam would be limited and the Assamese people would also not buy and read the book, because of two main reasons: firstly, they think they know everything about her and secondly, they think they are so important that they should get a free signed copy from the writer instead of buying it, assuming the writer was minting money in dollars from the sale of the book outside India.

Before I said something more, the gentleman became rather cross and remarked, "I was not expecting such an explanation from you for not publishing a book on her. I thought you will take my advice in the right spirit so that unsung heroes and heroines of Assam become famous outside Assam also."

He left the place in a huff. I am still wondering what I said wrong. Nevertheless, his advice ignited my inner feelings and I told myself, I might be blessed by the Almighty to complete the task with sincerity and I accepted it with folded hands as a precious gift to me and my family from the Almighty. At that moment I decided to write a book on the martyr.

To gather some first-hand information, I along with my wife, Monalisha Borah, my friend, Shri Aroopjyoti Das and few lovely ladies, visited the residence of the martyr at Barangabari, a village under Gohpur sub-division. I met her younger stepbrother, Shri Kalicharan Barua, his son Abhijit (Kaju) Barua and his other family members. We spent about two hours with them for a heart-to-heart talk. I got many insights into the life of the young martyr, particularly about her leadership qualities, patriotism and about her inner beauty as a great human being. Her brother told me about the day of her martyrdom, about how her body was cremated far away from the prying eyes of the British administration. He also talked about the martyrdom of Mukunda Kakati at the same site.

My mother, Late Dashami Borah, Head Pandit of Normal Practicing School was from Bihali, around thirty-five kilometres away from Barangabari, the birth place of Martyr Kanaklata

Barua. She was a few years older than my mother. My mother often used to describe her when I was a kid, "Kanaklata *baideu* (elder sister) had strikingly long hair which we used to admire. Even at the cremation ground there was a buzz amongst the ladies about her long beautiful black hair."

I cannot authenticate my mother's version nor reject her version. As the information on the martyr are taken from different sources, nothing can be authenticated and therefore I preferred to write a historical novel, instead of a biography on the martyr like I did for the Assamese icons Mula Gabharu and Abhayeshwari Devi, Queen of Bijni, a princely state of lower Assam. However, I have tried my best to uphold the dignity of Kanaklata Barua while portraying her as the protagonist of the novel. If any of the information hurts some of the readers, I submit my unconditional apology.

I am, first and foremost, thankful to the learned man who inspired me to write the book on Kanaklata Barua, inspite of his reluctance to provide any help. I was reminded of one of my friends who inspired me to write a book on Abhayeshwari Devi and then stopped communication with me once I had requested him to help me to find a publisher for the book. Once bitten and twice shy, I have not requested any of my friends to help me in the publication of this novel, as I do not want to lose more friends in the process of writing.

This novel may be a more humane portrayal, instead of the depiction of a martyr as a demigod. We see her having a family that was caring and supportive. To make an image larger than life, often human needs and realistic surroundings are overlooked. For example, even in an ordinary novel you'd rarely find the female protagonist suffering from diarrhea or the mention of a fart by the male protagonist. Similarly, whenever we read about an icon, seldom do we find casual conversations with his/her friends or squabbling between siblings. In one chapter, I try to dwell on her relation with her stepmother, which might be true or false; but I could not see any reason to believe that the quintessential relation between Kanaklata and her stepmother did exist, though I heard something otherwise from some of the locals as a college student during my visits to Barangabari and Gohpur.

Kanaklata as a young girl was like any other girl next door. However, she was relatively bolder and more patriotic than a girl of her age. Had she not been killed by a bullet that day, she would have died in obscurity after a few decades in independent India like many who might have been bolder and more patriotic, due to their poor socio-economic background. I have tried to portray her as a bold, helpful, patriotic girl till her attainment of martyrdom in 1942 at a very young age of seventeen.

However, being a proverbial sniffer dog, I wonder whether she was also a sacrificial goat for the influential leaders of India who had not lost any of their children in the Independence movement, but roosted the benefits accrued from all the movements including that of Indian independence. In many cases, these leaders had sent their children to a safe haven for their higher studies, much like the Hurriyat leaders are sending their wards to foreign countries for their higher studies, while instigating the poor Kashmiri students to pelt stones at the Indian Army and take the barrage of bullets in their chests. Or the leaders here who instigate the poor young men of the valley to take up guns against the Indian Army. Can you give me an example of a single leader of any generation, who had sent his or her child to lead a procession where there was the possibility of firing or a brutal lathi charge? Yes, you can say Lala Lajpat Rai was a victim of a brutal lathi charge; but at a ripe age he had led the procession himself. So, this question always haunted me: Was Kanaklata also an incidental heroine of the Independence movement of India after she was forced or brainwashed to lead the procession? Nobody can be sure; but criticising the intent of a martyr is not welcome by the masses led by groups of selfish leaders; as they know a discussion may expose their real faces and real intent before the public. After all, we all follow the golden rule of the elites: 'You scratch my back, I shall scratch yours.'

The writers and historians also praise the instigators (leaders of a movement) who have great eloquence to motivate common people to die for a cause. The common people in turn put the leaders at the helm of affairs after a successful movement to be cheated by them once again. Is there any remedy? Perhaps, we shall get a resounding 'no' as an answer to this question. However, once in a century, you may get a real leader who sacrifices everything for the people and also rules the hearts of the common people while occupying the highest post of a country.

Kanaklata was no doubt a young lady who had above average qualities of leadership and patriotism. My view on her leadership qualities has been bolstered because of the fact that during the same period, Assam had lost at least twenty other people who fell to British bullets, but remain unsung. Apart from a handful of local people, no one knows the names of the other martyrs apart from two – Mukunda Kakati (who was killed along with Kanaklata) and Bhogeswari Phukanani of Nagaon. Even the martyrs of the uprising of Patharughat and Phulaguri did not get any recognition. Therefore, we can very easily assume that she was much above average as far as leadership and patriotism were concerned. That she stood out even at such a young age. My work has also been built up on these assumptions which culminated in the attainment of Kanaklata's martyrdom unlike the others.

Although I know the name of the officer in charge of the Gohpur Police station and the police constable who fired upon Kanaklata and Mukunda Kakati that fateful day, I prefer not to mention their names for obvious reasons. I do not wish to make devils immortal along with the revered martyrs.

I hope this book will help the students of history to look at the history of Assam with a different perspective. Some portions of the book may be helpful to aspirants of different examinations conducted by different agencies across India for sections on the contemporary history of Assam during the freedom struggle of India.

Finally, I submit my unconditional apology once again for any omission and commission on my part while penning down this historical work.

Without tacit help from Dr Anjan Oja, Retired Principal of Chaiduar College, this book would not have been completed. He arranged my meetings with the family of Kanaklata, Smt Lokeswari Handique, an expert on Kanaklata's life and with Shri Nagen Konwar, another expert on the martyr. The help provided by Shri Paras Saikia of Ishan News, Shri Bikash Bora and his wife Mrs. Nabanita Bora are praiseworthy. I am also thankful to my old friend, Shri Aroopjyoti Das, Ms. Amrin

Sultana (who made a video on our discussion with the martyr's family at their residence) and Ms. Malabika Saikia, CEO of Man Pokhila, who accompanied my wife, Monalisha Borah and me on my first visit to Gohpur for this project. I am also thankful to Shri Sanjib Gohain Barua, IAS, an accomplished photographer of Assam who accompanied me to Patharughat and Dhekiajuli to click some beautiful photographs for the book. Shri Aroopjyoti Das gave me a day by accompanying me to Phulaguri as well. Not only did his company help me in my discussions with the local people of Phulaguri, he also helped me to take some photographs. I am thankful to him for giving me his valuable time.

Some of the content (deliberately I am not using the word 'facts') for my book has been taken from Wikipedia, Google searches and historical articles of some known and unknown authors. I am thankful to all of them.

Like my earlier books, this book is also written contextually and like in other books, deliberately I have written some of the facts more than once which prevents my readers from taking memory tests while reading the book.

As always, I am thankful to my readers, friends and my family members for their all-round support throughout my literary journey of more than four decades.

I am thankful to the residents of Barangabari, Phulaguri, Patharughat, Dhekiajuli and Gohpur for sparing their valuable time to discuss various incidents. I saw in their eyes pride and sorrow while discussing the tragedy, but also the moments of pride in the history of Assam.

I am also thankful to Shri D.K. Chouhan for providing me some very important inputs on tea garden communities.

However, above all, my gratitude to the Honourable PM, Modi ji for his inspiring pep talks encouraging people to write books on the unsung heroes and heroines of India.

Hiranya Borah

Basic Sources of Information

In this book, I try to find the background of that infamous firing incident that took place on the 20th of September, 1942 and the aftermath from different persons in Barangabari and Gohpur.

However, my mother, Dashami Borah, was the first informant, though her version was based on mostly hearsay from her father and her uncles. Her father, Kusharam Borah, along with her uncles had been beaten up black and blue by the stooges of the British Raj when they had tried to hoist the national flag at the Bihali police station which was situated about 40 kilometres away from the Gohpur police station. My mother recalled, how as an eight-year-old girl, she had witnessed the bloody faces of her father and her uncles after the violent lathi charge by the police on that particular day. Luckily no firing had taken place at the Bihali police station, unlike the two firing incidents that took place that day in Assam. Just for the record, Bihali police station is situated hardly half a kilometre away from my grandfather's residence at Niz Bihali.

Kanaklata Barua had lost her mother at a very early age and she had to be brought up by her stepmother. Her stepmother, Jonaki Barua was also blessed with a few children, the youngest of them being Shri Kalicharan Barua. When Kanaklata Barua was shot dead from point blank range by an Indian constable of the British Raj, Kalicharan Barua was about two and a half years old. According to him, he could not recollect what had happened that morning when his sister had attained martyrdom. However, he heard in detail about what had happened on that day from his elder sisters, friends of Kanaklata Barua, relatives and the persons present at the time of firing. He heard the horrific incident from so many different people who described it second to second, that he sometimes feels that he had witnessed it himself, making him the most reliable and authentic resource person for my book.

Smt Lokeswari Handique, an expert on Kanaklata's life and Shri Nagen Konwar, another expert provided me many valuable inputs for my book. Mrs. Konwar also gave me some inputs.

Dr. Anjan Oja was extremely knowledgeable about the life and exploits of Kanaklata Barua and was one of the most reliable resource persons for my book.

Young journalist, Shri Ishan Barua also provided information on the martyr and contemporary history of Gohpur and Barangabari.

One of my uncles, Shri Tanka Bora, in his nineties, also gave valuable inputs.

Shri D.K. Chouhan was also an important resource contributor. I also took some valuable information from '*Bharatar Swadhinata Andolanat Asomor Chah Gosthi/ Adivasir Avadan*' by Shri Nakul Kurmi.

Valuable inputs on the life of martyrs Kanaklata Barua, Mukunda Kakati, Bhogeswari Phukanani, and the martyrs of

Dhekiajuli, Patharughat and Phulaguri were shared by residents of Gohpur, Barangabari, Bihali, Patharughat, Dhekiajuli and Phulaguri during my visits.

I also visited the Cellular Jail to get an idea about the plight of the imprisoned freedom fighters during their confinement in the unhygienic cramped cells of the infamous Kalapani. The arrangements made to mete out punishment to the patriots will make you weep even today. Similarly, the instruments given to the prisoners for work, will send shivers down one's spine.

CONTENTS

CHAPTER-I
HARI HARA RAJKHOWA

The scar on his face, close to his left temple made his face somewhat frightening for me when I was a little kid of five. Slowly I started loving him for his sweet conversations while putting me on his lap whenever he visited our home. He was a distant relative of my mother who called my mother *Maakan* (young mom) while my mother addressed him as *Hari Dedai* (younger brother of her father). Slowly I became courageous enough to touch his scar, which was extremely smooth and red in colour. One day, when I was about seven years old, I dared to ask him how he had got the scar, expecting an answer that he had also been a naughty boy like me when he was younger.

However, with a smile he replied, "My son, it is not a scar, it is a symbol of pride. It is a symbol of my unadulterated love for my country."

I could not understand his response to my simple question on that day. However, I did not dare to ask him for an explanation.

One day when I was reading the poem, 'I ought to love my country' at the top of my voice, my mother told me that the scar on Hari Hara *koka* (grandpa) was a bullet injury he had received as a young man. He had been in the same procession with the great lady of their time, Kanaklata Barua who had made the supreme sacrifice for our motherland. On the fateful day of 20th September 1942, Kanaklata Barua and Mukunda Kakati were martyred at the west gate of Gohpur police station, while many more were injured. Hari Hara Rajkhowa was one of them. After independence of our country, he joined the central government as a post master and remained a bachelor. We used to call him 'koka' and he used to love us as though we were his grandchildren. As I grew older, I became very close to him.

Hari Hara koka was born to a wealthy farmer family of Barangabari in 1917, the same year of birth with the third Prime Minister of India, Indira Gandhi. Kanaklata Barua was also born in Barangabari to another rich family. He was about five years older than Kanaklata Barua.

Everyone knows the role of Indira Gandhi in the freedom struggle of India, but most of us are unaware of the contributions of the lesser mortals like Hari Hara Rajkhowa. Kanaklata Barua, Bhogeswari Phukanani, Mukunda Kakati's sacrifices are not well known either. So far as Assam is concerned, names of hardly ten martyrs out of at least two hundred who laid down their lives in the freedom struggle are known to the new generation.

Similarly, out of more than 700 martyrs of the anti-foreigners' movement of Assam during 1980-85, hardly ten names are known across the state. On the other hand, students' leaders and other leaders who were spear-heading the movement, roost the benefits accrued from the agitation without deporting even 750 illegal foreigners out of estimated 50 lakh foreign nationals they had claimed resided in Assam during that period of time. In fact, except change of hands of power, no gainful result has been accrued by the common indigenous people of Assam out of that agitation. On the other hand, due to the fruitless agitation, Assam had been pushed back in all the human indices by at least 20 years compared to other progressive states. Any informative Assamese person of that generation rues the bad luck of the Assamese people of losing an academic year along with many things including the loss of many young lives in lieu of 'absolutely nothing'.

Coming back to the early life of Hari Hara koka, he was sent to the local school at the age six and then to Cotton College for his graduation at the age of eighteen. He had been a very good student all along his school life. Unfortunately, before he could complete his graduation, he joined the Quit India movement responding to the call of the Father of the Nation. Because of his educational background and ability to convince the masses about the necessity to overthrow the British government, he became a student leader of a large area under the present Gohpur subdivision of Biswanath District, situated in the eastern part of Assam. This part of his life is known to everyone in his generation of that area, though the present generation doesn't seem to have heard of his name, let alone his contribution and sacrifice for our motherland during the Independence movement.

In 1980, during a long-forced holiday due to the Assam agitation against illegal foreigners, I was forced to stay home. It was a tragedy that all the common students had lost a full academic year. However, most of the well to do families had sent their wards to educational hubs outside Assam so that they didn't lose an academic year nor to face the bullets of the law enforcing agencies.

During that period of turmoil, Hari Hara koka visited our home and stayed with us for some days. At that time, he was a retired government employee void of any official duties. After discussing different topics, one day after our evening tea, I asked him, "Koka, will you mind if I ask you a question?"

"Why am I sensing you are going to ask me a question, probably nobody, including your teacher or parents, have dared to ask?" he looked at me awkwardly.

"If you do not want to answer, I shall not insist. But I do not know why, I have a feeling you are going to answer my question," I told him seriously.

He thought for a while and told me, "I was at your age when my life changed forever. Like you, I had many dreams. I was also a student leader like you. However, perhaps you are like Jeevan Hazarika, who became the Home Secretary of Assam after completion of his studies during the same period when I left my education midway. He was advised by his uncle with whom he had to stay after his father's death, that with or without the success of the Quit India movement, only qualified persons would be appointed in the high offices by the incumbent British government or by the new Indian government. Hazarika took his uncle's advice and did not leave his studies midway, unlike me. Eventually, he graduated from Cotton College and got his master's degree from Calcutta University. Subsequently, he joined the Assam Administrative Service and retired as the Home Secretary of Assam a few years ago. And look at me, I joined the Quit India movement and left my education midway. I became an assistant postmaster and retired as a postmaster from a small town. Just for the record I am saying, both of us had the same results in our intermediate examination." He heaved a deep sigh.

Perhaps he was correct in comparing me to Jeevan Hazarika. Though I was not advised by anyone, I went to Delhi University for my higher studies in the midst of the failed agitation realising that the leaders were going to betray the common innocent people who unconditionally believed them and blindly followed them to take active part in the agitation. Actually, I took the cue from the conversation between Hari koka and myself in the backdrop of the uncomfortable question I had posed to him that day.

I kept mum for few minutes as he was in deep thought and then he told me, "I do not know whether I should allow you to ask the question which I am anticipating." He stopped for a minute.

Then he started talking to me again, "Your mother is like my own daughter and therefore you came to my life as my own grandson. However, I have observed that at times, you behave like a matured man. I have come to know that you have taken many right decisions at the right time even when your parents were opposing some of the decisions you had made. I am sure you will be a successful man despite facing a lot of hurdles in your life. Further, I know that your hobby is to write stories on different topics and backgrounds. You also may be interested to write something on Kanaklata Barua and Mukunda Kakati someday. If you write about them, I am sure, you will write a paragraph or two on me as well. Therefore, I have decided to bare everything before you so that one day people may understand the agony of my life to some extent." He stopped there.

He asked me, "Do you want to know why I remained a bachelor?"

I nodded. I did not want to disturb him as he was deep in thought at that time so I stood up to leave. However, he gestured to me to sit.

He answered my question after a long thought. It was mostly 'one way traffic' for another two hours with some occasional sighs and a few drops of tears from his eyes.

The synopsis of his long narration was: he had loved a girl with long, thick and wavy hair. Her complexion was dark but she was tall and beautiful. However, he was not in love with her because of her physical beauty; but because of her love for her country, her helpful nature and her refusal to marry him and choosing her country's independence. Her refusal to marry him made her closer to his heart and when she left this world forever, he realised he had to live in this world all alone with only her memories.

After his retirement, I was told by my mother that he devoted his time to the service of the downtrodden of that area.

He died six years after that conversation between us when I was posted at Giridih, Bihar (now, Jharkhand) as an Assistant Director, at the National Sample Survey Organization. However, he was able to remind me at the time of my selection to Indian Statistical Service that his prediction about my career had come true. I met him at my residence after I had cleared my UPSC examination few years before his death. At that time, I found him hale and hearty and never thought that he would leave this world so early.

What was the precise answer of the old man to my pointed question? Why did he become so emotional while baring everything to me?

He considered me not only as his own grandson but also his friend despite the age difference of 45 years between us. According to his own version, nobody had dared to ask him that particular question. Was he sure that I'd be writing the story about the girl with long hair? Or did he want to tell the story to someone to ease out the burden of sorrow he was carrying for so many years? Or did he understand that I was the perfect foil to share his tragic life with the masses in due course of time. I do not know exactly why he had opened up before me. Whatever may be the reason for opening up that chapter of his life, I felt very happy to know everything about his love-life as a young man of twenty.

As the story will unfold before you, it is a tragic one of a person who had to remain a bachelor and had sacrificed everything for the motherland selflessly. Perhaps you will get all the answers to the questions that disturbed me for a long time. But I did not ask him any question that day directly except nodding my head to his query whether I wanted to know why he had not married anyone.

What he told me was a tragic story about a person who loved a beautiful girl without any earthly desire and without any reciprocal love. Through the story, I got all the answers to my questions, without having had to ask them.

Chapter-II
A Born Leader

Some people are born leaders; some become leaders by their efforts and some are made leaders by circumstances. Again, some people were able to make their presence memorable in history while some were part of history by accident. Kanaklata was a born leader as she had inherited the leadership qualities from her forefathers.

Kanaklata was born into the famous Barua family of historically important Barangabari area of erstwhile Darrang district of middle Assam. Barangabari, erstwhile Kalongpur, alias Madhya Chaiduar village, was under the Gohpur Police Station, around twelve kilometres west of present sub-divisional town, Gohpur. Madhya Chaiduar was a very important gateway between Arunachal Pradesh and Assam during the Ahom regime from 1228 to 1826. This was one of the major tax collection centres for the Ahom kingdom and therefore, this village was frequently visited by dignitaries of the Ahom kingdom. To provide security to the dignitaries, a protection force was permanently posted at Barangabari village by the kingdom since the middle of 16th century after arguably the greatest Ahom King, Suhungmung Dihingia Raja annexed the Chutiya kingdom in 1525 after annihilating the last Chutiya King, Niladhwaj alias Nitai, the cowherd king. After annexation of the Chutiya kingdom, the *duars* (gates) along the Arunachal border came under the control of Ahom kings till the British annexation of the Ahom kingdom in 1826 as a result of the Yandaboo Treaty between the Burmese King and East India Company of England.

Kanaklata's family were descendants of 'Dola Kashariya Barua' who was the chief of the special protection group of the king and other high-profile dignitaries of the kingdom while on their tours to the countryside. As a result of her lineage, Kanaklata was carrying the blood of ancestors who were fearless leaders and also experts in combat with or without arms.

Kanaklata was blessed to the couple, Krishnakanta Barua and his first wife, Karneswari Barua, to make them proud parents of the most famous martyr of Assam in the Indian Independence movement. She had made a legacy for herself which her ancestors would have been proud of, just like her successors who would be proud of her for all time to come.

Officially it is claimed that her date of birth was 22nd December, 1924, however, I have my doubts as the fact remains that during those days, no one care for the date of birth of a girl in rural India. Another point one may kindly understand is that counting and reporting of age of a person is different in rural Assam in comparison with the present statistical system of reporting. In rural Assam, if a person completes fifteen years, while reporting he will be reported as a sixteen-year-old person. Therefore, when her younger brother told me that she was seventeen-years old when she attained martyrdom, she actually might have been only sixteen and a few months. I hope to be excused for not agreeing to the popular belief that she was born on that particular date. Anyway, from the school records she was seventeen years at the time of her demise.

Her grandfather, Ghanakanta Barua and grandmother, Rohila Barua had seven sons and Krishnakanta was the eldest one. Ghanakanta Barua was an influential person of the entire Barangabari area. Being the eldest son, at the age of forty-two, Krishnakanta was also an important man in 1942.

Though she was born to a blue-blooded family, Kanaklata was unlucky as a daughter as she lost her mother at an early age and got a stepmother, Jonaki Barua within a short time of her mother's death. In a sense, her life was somewhat similar to the life of the legendry Ahom princess, Mula Gabharu who also lost many of her near and dear ones at a very early age. The death of her mother and subsequent entry of her stepmother in her life, certainly did not make the childhood of Kanaklata Barua an enviable fairy's life.

We can only assume the relation between a young girl and her stepmother, no matter how much we gloss over their relation. However, their intra-personal relation could not diminish the fire of patriotism in Kanaklata Barua and her indomitable spirit of fighting for the independence of the country.

Early Inspiration from Mula Gabharu and Jaimati Kuwori

The life of Mula Gabharu inspired Kanaklata Barua. She was told the story of Mula Gabharu and Jaimati Kuwori in piece meal by her grandfather. Who knows, Kanaklata Barua's supreme sacrifice for the country is linked with the supreme sacrifice of Mula Gabharu and Jaimati Kuwori for the motherland?

Mula Gabharu was the daughter of the Ahom king, Supimphaa. Trained in the art of warfare and the use of weapons, she married Borgohain Frasengmung, a famous Ahom warrior. She along with a few women warriors went to the battlefield, to avenge her husband's death. Her husband Frasengmung Borgohain had died in the battle against Turbak, a Mughal invader in 1532, and herself also sacrificed her life in the Battle at Dikarai.

Mula Gabharu was not merely the name of a princess of Assam, but also an inspiration for all Assamese to fight for the sovereignty of the motherland. Not only did she become immortal for the Assamese as an individual, she made that particular day immortal in the annals of the history of Assam as a glorifying day for all the Assamese mothers, sisters and wives. In fact, we bow our heads for all the ladies who sacrificed their lives on that day for the motherland and our hearts are filled with pride for the mothers, sisters and wives.

(You can read the detailed story of Mula Gabharu in Annexure VIII)

Sati Jaymati

Sati Jaymati, also known as Jaymati Kuwori, an Ahom Princess is one of those socio-historical figures who is part of the collective consciousness of the people of Assam to this day.

Throughout the last four centuries, and till today, she is remembered as a patriot and martyr, promoted as a national hero, cherished as a symbol of the ideal wife, mother and the adobe of feminine virtues. She is even worshipped as a divine incarnation.

Her importance in the socio-cultural life of the Assamese people has remained vital even in today's context. There are instances of her representation, in varied themes, in almost all forms of art and literature produced in Assam at different times, particularly during the last two centuries.

Jaymati was born in the middle of the 17th century to Lai Thepena Borgohain and Chandradaru in Madhuri Gohain Gaon, Sibasagar.

Jaymati was married to King Gadapani (Gadadhar/ Supatphaa), son of Gobar Roja of Tungkhungia family by Choklong (a tradition of Ahom) marriage.

Gadapani was young, handsome, dynamic and capable of taking appropriate decisions at appropriate time for the welfare of the people of his kingdom. Though he did not have any formal education as per chronicles of the Ahom history, he proved himself as an extremely worthy leader with political acumen and foresight.

When Gadapani was in the line of throne, Ahom King Sulikphaa alias Lora Roja on the advice of his greedy mentor, Ahom General Laluksola Borphukan wanted to amputate Gadapani. In Ahom custom, a prince without a body part cannot be a king.

Sensing trouble from the Ahom King Sulikphaa alias Lora Roja, Gadapani on the advice of his wife Jaymati, along with his two minor sons, Lai and Lechai fled to the Naga Hills (Nagaland) and took shelter in Nagaland for a few months. The English term of the word *Lora Roja*' means 'Boy King'. Sulikphaa became king at a tender age and that's why he was nicknamed as – Lora Roja.

The real name of Sulikphaa alias Lora Raja was Sarugohain. In 1679, Laluk Sola Borphukan was able to put him on the Ahom throne as a puppet king of Ahom Kingdom. In all practical purposes, Laluk Sola Borphukan became the real ruler of the

Ahom kingdom by proxy. By the way, for information, Laluk Sula abandoned Guwahati after the Battle of Saraighat 1671, in which his brother Lachit Borphukan defeated the Mughals decisively at Saraighat. He was appointed Borphukan by the Ahom King, Udayaditya Singha after the death of his younger brother in 1672. Then, Laluksola tasted the blood of power, and became a king maker on the wave of popularity of his younger brother, Lachit Borphukan, the most famous Ahom General of all time.

Without an iota of doubt, the period when Gadapani was forced to flee from his own land was one of the darkest periods in the history of Assam (1674-1681). During the inefficient rule of the young and immature king Sulikphaa, due to the manipulation of Laluk Sula Borphukan, as many as 27 eligible princes and princesses and two kings were murdered in cold blood.

There was complete lawlessness in Assam and the future looked grim with Gadapani being their only hope. It was imperative therefore for Gadapani and his two sons to escape from Lora Roja's dragnet. He was helped by the aristocrat of the opposing camp of Laluksola Borphukan and majority of the people of Assam during that period of time

When Lora Roja's soldiers were not able to arrest Gadapani, his wife Joymati Kuwori was summoned to the court and asked to reveal where Gadapani was hiding. Even the King himself asked the whereabouts of her husband. She feigned ignorance about her husband's whereabout.

On her refusal to reveal the hide-outs of her husband, she was taken to *Jarenga Pather* (a field named Jarenga) by the *Chaudung* (officials engaged to give punishment for gruesome crimes in the Ahom Kingdom) in the Sivsagar district of

Assam. She was tied to a *Kotkora* plant (a thorny plant) and she was subject to inhumane torture normally only reserved for hardcore criminals.

When Gadapani came to know about the inhumane torture meted out to his wife, he came to Jarenga Pather incognito as a Naga and requested Jaymati to divulge the whereabout of her husband to the tyrant King Lora Raja. However, she refused to divulge anything to the king and his officials and remained firm in her decision and did not budge to the request of her beloved husband in disguise of a Naga. Instead, she asked Gadapani to leave the place immediately. If on that day, her husband would have been caught and imprisoned, her dream of building an empire, with sound socio-economic and political conditions, with Gadapani as the King of the Ahom Kingdom would have failed.

When Joymati did not disclose her husband's whereabouts, the intensity of the oppressive inhumane punishment increased. Finally, the princess breathed her last on 27th of March 1680 in Jarenga Pather after 14 days of continuous physical, mental and psychological torture. This is how Joymati Kuwori protected her husband and the kingdom till her last breath from the evil eyes and ears of the tyrant king, Lora Raja and his evil mentor. Her sacrifice, love and responsibility for her husband and motherland are well known to all the persons of all the generations in Assam.

Jaimati's devotion to her husband and kingdom is admired by the people of Assam and she was given the title of *Sati*. She was able to save her kingdom and people from the atrocities of the young immature tyrant and soon after her death she became an icon for bravery and sacrifice. Her death in the hands of the *Choudungs* became a rallying point for the common people against the king. Her selfless sacrifice, patriotism, courage, truthfulness and pride made her an icon in the history of Assam. Her greatness might be lying in the manifestation of her selfless and sincere truthfulness, heroism, patriotism and self-respect. Her sacrifice was not merely to save her husband's life, but more importantly, to protect a patriotic future king who could restore peace and tranquillity in the entire Ahom Kingdom.

Her dream became a reality when Gadapani ascended the throne in 1681 in the wave of popularity that swept the tyrant king and his followers to the ultimate downhill. He assumed the name of King Gadadhar Singha. Unfortunately, as Jaymati berthed her last on the 27th of March 1680, she could not see her dream come true.

In 1697 A.D. Jaymati and Gadadhar Singha's eldest son, arguably the greatest King of Ahom Kingdom, Rudra Singha, also known as Lai before he became a king, built the Joysagar Tank at Sivsagar at the very place where his mother Joymati was tortured to her death.

Just for record, the tank was constructed within 45 days and it became the largest man-made tank of Assam. It is also the largest of all the tanks built by any king of the entire Northeast. It has an area covering 318 acres (1.29 km^2) of land, including its four banks, out of which 155 acres (0.63 km^2) is filled with fresh water. About 2 km-long earthen water pipeline was constructed for water supply from the tank to the Rangpur Palace (Kareng Ghar). It is claimed, the water level of the tank stays at 14 feet higher than the ground level even now.

Chapter-III
A Girl with Rare Qualities

Though Kanaklata was born into the relatively rich Barua family, she was an expert as far as household chores were concerned. She was an expert weaver of *gamochas* and *mekhela-chadars* as well. Mahatma Gandhi once praised the Assamese women for their ability to weave dreams in their clothes. Though during those days, the gamocha was not as famous as today, Kanaklata perhaps knew that one day the 'phulam gamocha' would be popular. She used to encourage the young girls to learn how to make motifs that included flowers and other pictorial embroidery on gamochas, chadars, mekhelas and *rihas.* By the time she entered into her teens, she became an expert weaver of the Eri chadar, an Assamese winter shawl, as well. She knew knitting with sufficient skill to make shawls and pullovers at hurricane speed. She was a skilled cook as well, which was certified by Padma Bhushan awardee, Pushpalata Das while praising Kanaklata Barua in one of her widely read articles. She was an expert in the preparation of all Assamese dishes and Assamese *pithas* and *ladus* as well.

As mentioned earlier, some leaders are born, some are made by circumstances and some are driven by passion. And in the case of Kanaklata Barua, it was patriotism. A very few have the combination of all the three. Kanaklata Barua was a born leader. She always liked to lead a team from the front from her early days in almost all the fields she had ventured during her short but eventful life of about seventeen years. It was in stark contrast with the mentality of some leaders of those days (and most of the leaders of the present generation), who eventually accrued all the benefits of an independent country – from getting awards to jobs for their children, from getting plots of land and seats in the coveted educational institutes for their wards. Top leaders of those days, who had never sent their wards out to join a procession where danger loomed large, not only got a ministerial berth or some other coveted post, but also ensured their children, grandchildren and even great grandchildren would be getting similar posts in independent India. That might be the main reason of India's backwardness even after getting its independence more than seven decades ago.

Her thought process was remarkably different from ordinary girls of those days. She never thought women were weaker than their male counterparts. She never thought girls were less intelligent than boys. She never thought girls were less innovative than their male counterparts. She always thought that given a chance, a lady could create wonders in different fields.

She always used to say, "No doubt we are physically weaker than our brothers and fathers, but we are not inferior to any males in our thinking processes and intellectual activities." She used to tell her sisters, peers and mothers about the story of the rabbit and the lion where the rabbit was able to kill the mighty lion because of his superior intelligence compared to the inferior intellect of the physically powerful lion. Her gifted storytelling and her proficiency in Sanskrit, made her a respected young lady across class, creed and gender. Her often-stated statement – '*Buddhir yasya, balam tasya, nirbudhasya kuto balam pashya singho madonmattah, sashakena nipatitah*' (Intelligence is more powerful than physical strength of a person; see how a king of the jungle lion had been vanquished by an intelligent rabbit.) – became very popular among the girls.

She would prophesise that modern education would have a cutting-edge over the brutal physical strength of a person. She always advocated for female education in rural Assam, even when literacy rates for the males were extremely low.

Had she not become a martyr, she could have been a good singer, perhaps. She had a melodious voice and she used to sing *borgeet, biya naam* and Bihu songs with grace and poise.

Kanaklata was known for her helpful nature. There were many instances, and they were particularly recalled after she died. One story goes, when she was promoted to class III, a poor boy of her class told Kanaklata that, as his father was not in a position to buy the books after his promotion from class II to class III, he was leaving the school. Without a second thought, she gave away all her new books to her classmate.

After donating the entire set of new books, when she returned home empty handed from her school, expectedly she got a good thrashing from her stepmother.

However, when her grandfather came to know about the incident, he was very happy to learn of his granddaughter's large-heartedness and helpful nature. He called his granddaughter close to him and said, "I am glad that you have rescued a child from dropping out of school. I shall give you money for your books once again. But to understand value of money, I shall not have any *tamul* for the next two months to recover the financial loss for your donation."

At that moment Kanaklata quipped, "Why should you sacrifice your mouth freshener for my action? Instead, I shall not take the new dress that you would have given me for Bihu."

The old man hugged his granddaughter realising that, perhaps god had blessed them with a special little girl who was destined to do something great. In the end, neither had to sacrifice their favourite things as Kanaklata's grandpa had only joked with the little girl. It was evident that the young girl was aware of the value of money.

Another instance was when an old lonely lady had fallen sick, there was no one present to look after her at night. Kanaklata was hardly fifteen years of age, but she volunteered to stay with her for the night against the will of her family. They were worried as the old lady was suffering from a contagious disease. Luckily, Kanaklata did not catch it though she tended to her for an entire week. When the old lady recovered, and became hale and hearty once again, she blessed Kanaklata with a prayer for immortality.

When the old lady came to know about the supreme sacrifice of Kanaklata, she reportedly said,

"I am the culprit for Kanaklata's untimely death as I had given her the boon of immortality. Now, I am sure she has attained immortality by leaving this world so early because of my blessings or because of my curse in disguise. I rue my luck. Why did I not stand by her, when the policeman fired upon her? Why I could not behave like Bhogeswari Phukanani to teach the policeman a lesson before my death and save Kanaklata from the bullet?"

Once Kanaklata had saved a young boy from drowning in a river during summer when the river was in full spate. The young boy who did not know swimming, went to the deeper part of the river by mistake. Kanaklata was returning from school and saw that the boy was drowning as his friends were screaming for help. She jumped straight into the swelling river and being an excellent swimmer, she was able to rescue the boy from the jaws of death. No doubt, she got few more blessings for immortality from the parents of the boy as well.

There were many similar stories in circulation after her martyrdom on the morning of 20th September, 1942. Many might be based on facts and many fictitious. Nevertheless, such stories are generated for only great people and in my opinion, she was one of the greatest icons of Assam.

Chapter-IV
The Speaker

Kanaklata was also a wonderful speaker. She was said to be very particular about use of words, which were simple but very powerful. She used to speak on two personalities of Assam quite often to the people of nearby villages; they were Srimanta Sankar Deb and Haldhar Bhuyan, the Gandhi of Nagaon district. The synopses of her speeches have been reproduced in the following two sub-chapters.

Though, I am sure, the youngsters of the present generation are somewhat familiar with not only the name of Srimanta Sankar Dev but also have some knowledge of his unbound qualities and unparalleled work as a religious leader, social reformer and as an artist of the highest order.

Haldhar Bhuyan was not only an ardent follower of Shri Shri Sankar Dev, but also a social worker, who worked tirelessly for the downtrodden people of Nagaon. Though, today he may be an unknown entity for the present generation outside erstwhile Nagaon district, his domain of social work and political activities; tomorrow he may also become an icon of Assam after his work devoted to the people of Assam in general, and Nagaon district in particular is recognised.

The synopsis of her speech in Assamese on Srimanta Sankar Dev.

I am always fascinated by Srimanta Sankar Dev, our beloved and most respected Assamese icon, starting from the spelling of his name in English to his extraordinary personality. But what are the exceptional qualities that I know about him? Perhaps, I know very little about him or of any of the qualities he had possessed. Every time I read about him in some book and every time I hear about him from someone knowledgeable about him; I find something new about his un-paralleled persona.

I researched about almost all the famous religious gurus of all time. He outlived (119 years, 26th September, 1449 to 23rd August, 1568) all the famous religious gurus by miles, except a few mythological gurus of Sanatan Dharma, like Veda Vyas or the Dev Guru Brihaspati or Daitya Guru Shukracharya as they're said to be immortal. He started his educational journey quite late compared to other great persons of the world. He started his formal education at the age of twelve, which was four years more than the lifespan of Suka Muni, who reportedly died at the age of eight.

He was physically very strong unlike the other studious people. He had a flexible body of a good ballet dancer with enormous physical power; reportedly he had tamed a rogue bull when he was merely a teenaged boy. His body flexibility and physical strength combined, might be next only to Bhagwan Shri Krishna, the eternal hero of all time for the followers of Hinduism.

He was the original modern social reformer who aimed at making an egalitarian Assamese society, who used to walk in the Brahmaputra valley like a lion with a black mane covering his broad shoulders. He was the first person who tried to make a casteless Assamese society.

Except his Muslim follower Chandsai, a Muslim tailor who used to serve the Koch king as the royal tailor, nobody has claimed to see him in his true avatar with four hands. Though the Muslim tailor became a true follower of Srimanta Sankar Dev in due course of time, the great man never tried to convert him from a devout Muslim to become a Hindu. In other words, Srimanta Sankar Dev had never been a Hindu bigot per se. In the process, he laid the foundation of a larger Assamese society, free from religious bigotry and a society relatively free from untouchability a few centuries ago compared to other states of India even today.

He was a born leader who earned thousands of followers during his lifetime and even today, crores of people are following his ideals without raising any doubt about his intent, teachings and ideals.

He was a great lyricist of Borgeet who could make a mythical web by choosing appropriate words at the appropriate place through his numerous garlands of poetry. His voice was so soothing as he recited verses in the religious congregations early in the morning and during sunset, that thousands of ailing persons reportedly came to hear him to get some solace in the enchanted air around him and forget their pain.

He was a great storyteller and a great composer of epics in a new language, Brajavali, hitherto unknown to all around him but easily understandable to all the common people who were not conversant with the language of the elite, Sanskrit. He was an actor of high quality and a playwright director of high calibre. He introduced a new form of dance drama, Bhaowna, an invaluable gift to the Assamese society. He was an excellent script writer with impeachable dialogue writing capacity.

His contribution to the cultural field was epoch-making and till now, no critic questions his contribution. Satriya dance is a recognised and highly praised 'classical dance form' of modern India.

He was married twice, to Suryavati and Kalindi and had a contended family life. But without having any earthly attachment to anything in the world of death. He used to take the patronage of kings – Maharaj Nara Narayan being the main patron of Srimanta Sankar Dev – or the barons for conservation, publicity and penetration of his religious beliefs amongst the masses. Even then he was able to lead a life of a monk with austerity and without enjoying any personal comfort in the palaces of the kings. However, like many other religious leaders, he had also faced death threats which prompted him to hide in different places before his final settlement in Koch Behar.

In a nutshell, he was a multifaceted personality, a visionary who was much ahead of his time (Fifteenth and sixteenth century) about whose life and philosophy, like many, I also know very little so far.

The synopsis of her speech in Assamese on Lok Sewak Haldhar Bhuyan, 'Gandhi of Nagaon' translated into English

Lok Sewak Haldhar Bhuyan, known as the 'Gandhi of Nagaon' was born on 28th September, 1891 at Tetelisara village of Kampur in Nagaon district. He lost his parents, Babul Bhuyan and Sulabha Bhuyan at a very early age and had to be brought up by his uncle, the elder brother of his father, Madan Bhuyan. His daughter Phunsaki Bhuyan played the role of a mother to Haldhar Bhuyan as a young kid.

He started his schooling at Tetelisara primary school, reportedly at the age of eleven (one year earlier than Srimanta Sankar Dev started his education) taking interest in studies, inspired by his two studious elder cousins. He had completed his high school from Nagaon Government School. Later on, he began his college education at Cotton College, Guwahati in 1914 where he met Pandit Krishna Kanta Handique as his peer. As good friends, they used to hold a 'mock university' where K.K. Handique used to play the role of a VC and Haldhar Bhuyan used to play the role of a Registrar. However, the college education of Haldhar Bhuyan was short lived and he had to drop out in 1915 due to acute financial constraints. He joined as an assistant English teacher in a school. Later he worked as a clerk (Nakal Nobis – an official who is entrusted to copy the court proceedings) in the court and finally he joined as an assistant in the Nagaon Civil Hospital to fulfil the financial obligation towards his family. However, he left government service in 1921 and joined the Congress party.

He was married to Parbati in 1926; but unfortunately, she died in 1928 due to some incurable ailment. Due to family pressure in 1929, he remarried his sister-in-law, Mrinalini alias Aruna. The couple were blessed with eight children in due course of time. When he left this world in 1968, he left behind a host of children and grandchildren along with an unparalleled legacy of a social reformer.

It is said, at the early of age of fifteen, he got the first taste of social discrimination when he was not allowed to play phakua (Holi) at the Batadrawa, the birth place of Srimanta Sankar Dev. It is ironical that Srimanta Sankar Dev, who wanted to abolish the caste discrimination from the Assamese society long ago in the sixteenth century itself, could not perhaps influence his followers to follow his teachings in the true letter and spirit even at his own birth place. It was the defining moment for young Haldhar Bhuyan who vowed to dedicate his life to social justice, upholding equality and equity in the Assamese society. That culminated in forming the Sankar Sangha as one of the founders. He was the president of Sankar Sangha in 1930, 1931 and 1932.

Like any other youth of the pre-independence era, being an educated young man, he joined the Congress party and climbed the ladder of hierarchy of Congress leadership. Before he crossed the age of 30, he made a niche for himself as a socio-political leader of Nagaon district. However, God perhaps wanted to test his mettle as a great leader and organiser and he was put to test in 1921 at the age of 30.

In 1921, Gandhiji along with a few big shots of the

Congress, was on a visit to Assam. Nagaon was not in his original itinerary. A group of young leaders from Nagaon thought that Gandhiji's visit would galvanise the party workers of Nagaon to dedicate their lives for the country. With his strong and articulate arguments, Haldhar Bhuyan was able to convince the Father of the Nation, Mahatma Gandhi to deliver a lecture at Nagaon at his convenience. A date and time for his address was finalised. However, Haldhar Bhuyan and his followers had to face another big hurdle to cross before conducting of the scheduled public meeting at Nagaon. This time hurdle was created by the district administration. They summarily rejected the application for holding a public meeting at the district public field to be addressed by Mahatma on the grounds that the address by Gandhiji might vitiate the political atmosphere of the district.

The challenge to find an alternative venue for holding a mammoth rally was almost impossible. But there is a saying – gold shines when it is put into fire. Haldhar and his dedicated team decided to clear a forest full of 'chorat plants' to hold the meeting. The chorat plant is a common plant found in the jungles of Assam in abundance with uneven rough leaves. The leaves of the plants cause severe irritation and rashes whenever they come into contact with human skin. As decided, with the help of thousands of dedicated volunteers, he was able to clear the forest a night before Bapuji's lecture. The lecture was delivered by the Father of the Nation in the new field, in front of more than one lakh people, much to the unease of the district administration. This act of bravery and determination made Haldhar Bhuyan a household name in the entire Nagaon district. As a retaliatory action, district administration arrested Haldhar Bhuyan and put him behind bars for six months. When he came out of the jail, a leader was born.

He was not only a renowned freedom fighter, but also a great visionary. His tenure as a clerk in the Civil Hospital as a young man gave him an insight into how common men and women had to lose their eyesight untimely due to lack of basic medical facilities for the poor. At that age, he vowed to do something for the poor so that they'd have healthy eyesight like their rich counterparts. It was not a very easy task as he himself was not a medical practitioner. He studied Ayurveda in his free time, between his extremely busy schedule of organising rallies for national leaders in Nagaon and its adjoining districts, working for the Sankar Sangha and raising his voice against the atrocities committed against the downtrodden people, either by the British administration or by the affluent classes. Again, there is an old saying – while others think if punished, the person will suffer, a great person thinks god has given him an opportunity to do something great for himself and for the people. In case of Haldhar Bhuyan, when he was jailed by the British administration as punishment for leading a movement in the district following Mahatma Gandhi's call, he thought he was given an opportunity by the almighty to study Ayurveda to serve the poor people of Assam. Once he was able to garner the basic knowledge of medication in Ayurveda, he was more than convinced to start something big and be an organiser in the medical field. The rest was destiny for the poor people of the district (or for that matter for the people of Assam as a whole) who now had hope that they could have their eyesight intact for a few more years at an affordable cost.

As on today, we all know that he was the brain behind the foundation of Sankar Mission Eye Hospital of Nagaon district and was the first President of the Sankar Mission. and he remained at the helm of affairs of the mission for a long time. There are countless poor people of Assam and other north-eastern states that have benefitted from the yeoman services of the mission for the last few decades.

Other than the Sankar Mission, he was involved in the leprosy eradication mission, in providing medical assistance to TB patients and the establishment of better medical facilities for the maternity and pediatric patients in the Nagaon district. In addition, he was instrumental in establishing an orphanage at Nagaon.

Now let us discuss his contribution in the socio-religious field of Assam. The conflict between the Brahmanical system and the Ek Saraniya Vaisnavite religion propagated by Srimanta Sankar Dev had started more than three hundred years ago without a clear winner. The students of history knew that though after fall of Chutiya kingdom of Upper Assam in 1525, politically the Ahom kingdom became stronger and was the undisputed sovereign of almost the entire Assam for almost 600 years (1228-1826). But the Ahom kingdom had to adopt the Chutiya culture unwittingly and that fortunately became the foundation of modern Assamese society. In a similar analogy, in the contest of superiority of the two religious systems, apparently in the number game, the followers of Sankar Dev are much ahead of the followers of the Brahmanical system in Assam. But what is the ground reality? Most of the Assamese people follow the Brahmanical caste system in letter and spirit till today. Therefore, the fundamental spirit of making a casteless egalitarian society among the followers of Sankar Dev is a distant reality even today. However, till a few decades ago, the caste system was rampant. Chandra Prabha Saikiani was a victim of the caste system that prevailed in those days. Had she been an ordinary lady, she would have been broken into pieces. But she fought back and became an icon for the modern Assamese society. Haldhar Bhuyan also got a taste of caste based discrimination as a teenager. Even today, whether we publicly admit or not, an inter-caste marriage among the Assamese people is a rare event. Degrading to the lower caste in the case of an inter-caste marriage was a very common phenomenon even few decades ago. Haldhar Bhuyan and few like-minded people were instrumental in abolishing this system partially over the years. But even today, no one from upper caste wants to abolish the caste system, though most of them are vocal against the reservation policy of the government in the education sectors and in the job markets on the basis of caste and creed. That is the reality of today's modern Assam. Again, whether public admission is there or not, even the highest seat of authority of Ek Saraniya Vaishnavite religion, Majuli, is not free from rampant caste discrimination. Any discussion about caste discrimination in Majuli is taboo due to socio-political reasons. But the fact remains, due to rampant caste discrimination in Majuli, a sizable number of tribal population is converting into Christianity. So, can we say the Brahmanical system has the last laugh in the battle of superiority between the two conflicting religious systems?

Coming back to the enormous contribution of Haldhar Bhuyan in reducing the caste discrimination almost a century ago. By establishing Sankar Sangha through his initiatives, he actually reduced the hegemony of the upper castes in the Vaishnavite movement in Assam up to a large extent. As the Sankar Sangha is growing by leaps and bounds, the hegemony of the satras has drastically came down as far as religious matters are concerned, though culturally they are still a force to be reckoned with. Among the educated masses, the religious influence of the satras became a non-entity though they are surviving due to political compulsions. All these developments happened slowly due to the untiring efforts of many social leaders and Haldhar Bhuyan was, perhaps, the most important leader among others in the Nagaon district in the early and middle part of the 20th century.

As already stated earlier, he was one of the founding members of the largest religious organisation in Assam – Sankar Sangha. But recently, Sankar Sangha has been facing criticism of being an organisation that is dividing the Assamese society further and is damaging the colourful fabric of Assam. If it is so, the officials of this organisation should introspect their line of action in the light of the sacrifice of Haldhar Bhuyan and his associates who toiled to make a larger egalitarian Assamese society free from religious bigotries and from the oppressive caste system that prevails even today in larger parts of rural Assam.

As a whole, his contributions to modern Assamese society is arguably epoch making with far-reaching effects.

Chapter-V
Winds of Change

The Independence Movement of India was in full throttle in Assam just as it was in the other states of India when Kanaklata Barua was born in 1924.

Mahatma Gandhi was the undisputed leader of three major campaigns in the Indian Independence Movement: he launched the Non-cooperation movement in 1919-1922, then he led the Civil Disobedience movement and the Salt Satyagraha of 1930-1931, and finally, he called for the Quit India movement during 1940-1942.

It was during the Quit India movement that Kanaklata Barua attained martyrdom, which was reportedly eulogised by Rup Konwar Jyoti Prasad Aggarwal through its main character in his play *Labhita.*

The Quit India movement of 1942, also known as the August Kranti movement was launched at the Bombay session of the All-India Congress Committee at the behest of Mahatma Gandhi on 8th August 1942, during World War II, with a demand for the British to leave India forever.

The very next day, Gandhiji and other leaders of the country were arrested by the British government and put behind bars. Due to lack of proper leadership at the ground level, the demonstrations against the arrest of top leaders became disorderly, but remained mainly non-violent throughout the country in the following days.

By the middle of 1942, Japanese troops reached Nagaland after over-running Manipur, in eastern borders of India. Pressure was mounting on British administration from the United States as well to solve the issue of the future status of India before the end of the war.

In March 1942, the British Prime Minister, Winston Churchill, sent Sir Stafford Cripps, a member of the War Cabinet, to India to discuss the British Government's Draft Declaration with Indian Congress and other stakeholders. The draft proposed to grant India Dominion status after the war was over conceding few changes to the British Government Act of 1935. The draft was summarily rejected by the Congress Working Committee in its meeting. The failure of the Cripps Mission further widened the differences between the Congress and the British government.

The failure of the Cripps Mission along with the general frustration with the British administration in India and the news of advances of the Japanese troops in south-east Asia emboldened Gandhiji to call for a voluntary British withdrawal from India. From the 29th of April to the 1st of May 1942, the All-India Congress Committee congregation was held in Allahabad to discuss the resolution of the Working Committee. Although Gandhiji was not present in the meeting, some of his points were admitted into the resolution. The most significant point by Gandhiji that was taken into consideration was the commitment of the committee to maintain non-violence at any cost. On the 14th of July 1942, the Congress Working

Committee met again at Wardha and resolved that it would authorise Gandhiji to take charge of the non-violent movement for full-fledged independence. The resolution, popularly known as the 'Quit India' resolution, was placed before the All-India Congress Committee meeting held on the 7th and 8th of August 1942. The Committee approved the resolution.

Gandhiji appealed to all the people from all the geographical and social entities to join the movement with the underlying promise of 'Do or Die' for the independence of the motherland. After the arrest of the leaders under the Defence of India Rules, the Working Committee, the All-India Congress Committee and the four Provincial Congress Committees were declared unlawful associations under the Criminal Law Amendment Act of 1908. Holding of public meetings was prohibited under rule 56 of the Defence of India Rules. The arrest of Gandhiji and the Congress leaders led to mass demonstrations throughout the country. Thousands were martyred and injured in the wake of the Quit India movement in the subsequent months. Wild cat strikes were also called in many places. The British administration was able to suppress many of these demonstrations by different violent means. More than 100,000 people were imprisoned during this period with or without any judicial scrutiny.

The success of the Quit India movement, can be gauged by how it unified the Indian people against the British rule. Though most of the demonstrations had been quelled by the British administration using ruthless power by 1944, the fire for independence had already been ignited in the heart of each Indian by that time. After his release from his confinement in 1944, Gandhiji became optimistic of achieving the goal of independence. He felt that it was the appropriate time to push forward his demand for independence and he continued the pressure, taking different steps. To press his demand for independence, at a personal level, he took up his famous 21-day fast against the will of the fellow top leaders including Pt. Jawaharlal Nehru who were worried about his health at the age of 75.

In the meantime, winds of change in the world order were taking the shape of a typhoon. As a result, by the end of the World War II, Britain lost its pivotal place in the world order politically and militarily to the emerging power USA. In fact, after few years, the British power was pushed to a further lower position in the world order. USA started dictating what should be the political order in the world. In fact, what USA pleaded to the European powers few years ago turned into 'advice' from USA, if not an 'order'. The British government could not ignore the long pending demand for Independence by the Indian people. In the meantime, British Prime Minister, Churchill – who was dead against Indian independence – lost the election to the labour party headed by Atlee, who was willing to concede the demand of total independence of India. Therefore, many historians think, it was not because of the freedom struggle led by the Congress party, but because of the rise of Hitler in the late thirties of the previous century and his (Germany's) loss to the Allied Forces led by USA in the World War II that led to India's Independence. To bolster their arguments, they cite the examples all the colonies of Africa and Asia, getting independence one by one, without any organised freedom struggle in those countries. Whatever may be the 'main reason' of getting independence by our country, we cannot ignore the participation and sacrifices of the common people of India in the freedom struggle.

Like people of any other states of India, the people of Assam also played an important role in the freedom struggle. In Assam, the anguish against the British Raj came into the forefront in the first half of the 19th century. Assam came under direct British rule after the Treaty of Yandaboo between the East India Company of England and Burmese King without any representation from Assam in 1826. Since then, many people of Assam belonging to both the aristocracy and the masses have fought for freedom from British rule.

Gomdhar Konwar was the first person from the Ahom dynasty who revolted against the East India Company just after annexation of Assam to its fold. He was assisted by Kandura Deka Phukan, Dharmadhar, Haranath and others from Ahom aristocracy. However, since this movement was not an organised one, the British was able to crush it easily, but failed to suppress the burning desire to breathe freely in the hearts of the people of Assam.

After a few years, another revolt was orchestrated by Piyali Barphukan. Incidentally, Piyali Barphukan was the patriotic son of the unpatriotic Badan Barphukan, who brought the Burmese army to fulfil his desire to rule Assam by proxy. Piyali Barphukan, with the help of Jiuram Dulia Barua, Benudhar Konwar, Rupchand Konwar and a few other patriots, he attacked the British camp at Rangpur. Initially, they were successful in their attempt to over-run the camp. But eventually, they were captured by the British army. After following a sham judicial procedure, Piyali Barphukan and

Jiuram Dulia Barua were hanged to death. The rest of the patriots were jailed for fourteen years in different jails.

With logistic support from a lower-level Indian British army personnel, another plot was hatched by a patriot, Gadadhar Gohain against the British administration. According to that plan, they drew a blueprint to kill all the British officials posted in Upper Assam. However, the British Army came to know about the plot before it could be executed by the patriots. Gadadhar Gohain was captured and imprisoned for life.

In 1857, when the first major (somewhat Pan-India and somewhat organised) revolt (many touted it as it was the first freedom struggle of India) against the British rule took place, tea planter, Maniram Dewan revolted against the British. He visited Kolkata and was in constant touch with the last Ahom king, Kandarpeswar Singha and his advisor, Piyali Barua. They planned to attack the British army under the leadership of the Ahom king, Kandarpeswar Singha. Unfortunately, the attempt to overthrow the British hegemony failed and the British captured and imprisoned many of the patriots. Maniram Dewan was arrested in Kolkata. The British also arrested Kandarpeswar Singha and imprisoned him for treason. Some of the arrested freedom fighters were deported to Andaman Island, known as 'Kaliapani' or 'Kalapani' in those days. On 26th February, 1858, Maniram Dewan and Piyali Barua were hanged to death in Jorhat jail for 'high treason' against the British government.

Three years after the hanging of Maniram Dewan and Piyali Barua, in 1861, a peasant uprising took place at Phulaguri in Nagaon district where a good number of people were martyred (details in Annexure-V).

In 1894 another peasant uprising took place at Patharughat in Darrang District. The British Police ruthlessly killed 141 peasants and maimed hundreds of innocent people, making it a black day in the history of Assam (details in Annexure-VI).

After the formation of the Indian National Congress in 1885 and the subsequent agenda formulated by the congress, Assamese people also got a platform to fight for their independence albeit as an 'integral part of India', not as 'Independent Assam'.

As we all know, the emergence of Gandhiji as the undisputed leader of the Congress preceded the most important phase of freedom struggle of India. The freedom struggle in Assam also gained momentum after Gandhiji's visit to Assam in 1921 and his subsequent visits to Assam. Congress volunteers in thousands joined the Non-cooperation, Civil Disobedience and other movements along with other parts of India.

Though most of the freedom-loving people of Assam joined the non-violent movement led by Mahatma Gandhi, a few youths joined armed movements to oust the British militarily.

Chandranath Sarma, Nabin Chandra Bordoloi, Tarun Ram Phukan, Gopinath Bordoloi, Amiyo Kumar Das, Jyotiprasad Agarwal and few others took on the mantle of the Indian freedom struggle in Assam.

On 9th August, 1942, when Gandhiji from the platform of Indian National Congress urged the Indian people to associate themselves with the Quit India movement, people of Assam also took part in it in large numbers whole heartedly. Gopinath Bordoloi, Bishnuram Medhi, Fakhruddin Ali Ahmed, Amiyo Kumar Das, Jyotiprasad Agarwala, Hem Barua, Bijoy Chandra Bhagwati, Chandraprabha Saikiani, and Pushpalata

Das led the movement in Assam. The Socialist party under the leadership of Jayaprakash Narayan in Assam also took part in the freedom struggle. However, the Communist Party of India (CPI) opposed the popular movement and rather supported the British government. Contrary to that, the Revolutionary Communist Party of India (RCPI) supported the freedom struggle of the people of India.

During the movement Kushal Konwar was hanged for alleged subversive activities against the British government by derailing a passenger train near Sarupathar. The incident had been eulogised by Dr. Birendra Kumar Bhattacharya in his Jnanpith award winning novel, *Mritunjay.* (Details of Martyr, Kushal Konwar is in Annexure-III.)

Kanaklata Barua, Mukunda Kakati, Bhogeswari Phukanani, Mangal Kurmi, Maniram Kachari, Hemoram Pator, Gunabhi Bordoloi, Lerela Boro, Ratan Kachari, Lakhi Hazarika, Thagi Sut, Boloram Sut, Madan Barman, Rauta Boro, Nidhanu Rajbangshi and many others made their supreme sacrifices by taking bullets in their chests in 1942. Their martyrdom did not go in vain as we got our independence less than five years after their sacrifice.

Unlike the leaders of CPI, Bishnu Prasad Rabha, Haren Kalita, Haridas Deka, Khagen Barbora, Mathura Deka, Gobinda Kalita, Chatrasing Teron, Chintaharan Kalita, Nirendra Lahiri, Uma Sarma, Suresh Bhattacharya, Sarat Rabha, Mohanlal Mukherjee, Hena Ganguli of RCPI not only took part in the freedom struggle of India, but also inspired lakhs of people to join the movement through their fiery speeches and eye-catching cultural programmes.

It is worth mentioning that, while the common people of India were taking part in the Quit India movement, one of the greatest sons of India, Netaji Subhas Chandra Bose attacked the British imperial forces from outside with his Azad Hind Fauj or the Indian National Army (INA). The INA tried to enter Indian mainland through the eastern borders of Assam with the help of the Japanese army. They were able to liberate Moirang in Manipur and almost liberated Kohima in Nagaland. However, they failed to capture Nagaland and their progress was halted by the British army at the periphery of Kohima in Nagaland.

So far as specific contributions of Kanaklata Barua in the freedom struggle of India was concerned, she had been a local level young dynamic leader who influenced the local ladies irrespective of their age to join the Quit India movement till she attained her martyrdom. Her death galvanised all the youths, irrespective of gender to fight for the independence of India which culminated in achieving the main goal of driving out the British peacefully in 1947. After Independence on 15th August, 1947 to commemorate her martyrdom, the Government of Assam declared 20th September as Martyr's Day, and every year it is observed to remember all the martyrs. She is a legend and an idol for many youngsters who want to serve the country even today.

Chapter-VI
A Decisive Young Beauty

It is also believed that her request to join the 'Mrityu Bahini' (sacrificial/death brigade) was not granted by the senior leaders like Padma Bhushan, Pushpalata Das. However, many have contradicted this version. It is claimed that as she was very young at that time, and therefore, she was not allowed to lead the procession to hoist the tricolour flag at the local police station as a part of a national programme to hoist flags at the rooftop of each and every police station across the country. It is said that only due to her insistence, she was allowed to join Mrityu Bahini and allowed to lead the procession that day. According to the leader of the stature of Pushpalata Das, it was due to her insistence to join the brigade and to lead the procession on the fateful day, that the reluctant leaders had to concede her demand.

In a book, after Kanaklata's death, Padma Bhushan Pushpalata Das had written:

'Sweet Kanaklata came out when I went to her village when she disclosed her intention to join the death brigade.

"Baideu, I cannot keep out something from my inner mind that has been urging me. You should not prevent me from joining." (Reproduced from the book, *Asomor Mahiyashi Nari* written by Smti. Lokeswari Handique.)

According to Pushpalata Das, due to the rock-solid confidence in her approach, despite her young age, Kanaklata Barua was allowed to join the Mrityu Bahini. Unlike most of the other leaders, Kanaklata wanted to lead from the front instead of staying away from the scene of the 'actual action', so she volunteered to lead the procession of Barangabari to Gohpur police station which was thirteen kilometres away.

It is also said that she had never feared to go alone at night for organisational work of the independence movement. She had never given any excuse for not taking any responsibility both at the household level or societal level. Rather she always asked for more responsibilities which were at par with her male counterparts.

Kanaklata Barua was perhaps one of the rare persons who was able to inspire people for a noble cause and had guts to lead a procession where death would loom large over their heads. Not fearing any danger, she chose to lead when the leaders of any conflict shied away from real actions but inspired others to go to the real line of action.

On 20th September, 1942, she could have avoided leading the procession like most of the state level and local level leaders (those who were not arrested till that day) and even after that, she could have handed over the duty of carrying the flag once the 303 rifle was pointed at her chest for more than ten minutes before the fatal firing. While talking to the British police, neither did she lose her cool nor showed any sign of fear of death during the last ten minutes of her life. She stood out with her calm composure and her bravery, facing death square in the face. And that she was only a teenager at that time speaks volumes about her maturity and inherent leadership qualities. That might be the reason why she received the limelight and accolades at her martyrdom compared to the scores of martyrs who also sacrificed their lives on the same day.

I salute Kanaklata Barua for her exceptional courage and I put her on the highest pedestal as a leader of exceptional leadership qualities. I put her ahead of the leaders who inspired people, but shied away from leading a procession where death was imminent; no matter how many awards they were conferred upon or no matter what position they had attained in the government after independence.

Chapter-VII
One Sided Love Affairs

Whether you love me or not,
Whether you accompany me or not,
In the journey of my life,
I have to move on.
Your rejection,
My inspiration,
Both are precious 'Gifts of God',
As fuel of my high-speed engine,
That may drop me at the station,
God must have fixed much before my birth.

One loved only the motherland while the other loved both the motherland and the girl of sweet sixteen who could not think about anyone other than the freedom of her chained motherland. The young girl decided to sacrifice everything to make free her motherland from the British occupation. One who loves someone from the core of the heart understands that 'if one loves someone, he or she should not expect anything from the counterpart, even pure love on a reciprocal footing'. When the counterpart knows about the unadulterated love for her or for him, she or he tries to make the counterpart understand that though his/ her love is respected, she/ he has no option but to reject the proposal with all humility. So was the case with Hari Hara Rajkhowa and the young lady with long beautiful hair.

Hari Hara Rajkhowa might not have been the only one who had loved the young lady with long hair, with a beautiful physique and with an amicable nature; but also, with a stubborn attitude for the right cause. She was a beautiful lady by any standard in the eyes of dozens of eligible youths of that area of that era. However, perhaps, Hari Hara was the only one who preferred to remain a lover for that young lady even after her martyrdom. He remained a bachelor till his last day. He never thought about himself as a jilted lover; rather he was proud to be the lover of an icon of Assam who had never reciprocated his love.

I wanted to know from him whether people of that area knew about his one-sided love affair with the beautiful lady with long hair. When he said 'yes' to my query, I had put forward my second question, "When?"

"I am not sure when people came to know about my one-sided love affair with her. But I started talking about her, my unadulterated love for her and her rejection of my proposal only after her death in the hands of British police," he answered thoughtfully.

"Did your parents not pressurise you to marry in the subsequent years?" I asked him as though I was a friend forgetting he was 45 years older than I or I was perhaps questioning him like a journalist bereft of any emotion.

"Yes, I had to withstand a lot of pressure from my parents and my close relatives in the next two decades. But her memory was so strong, I could not even think of marriage during my youthful days. Even now I feel her presence whenever I am alone," he confided like a friend.

"Didn't your close friends make fun of the whole issue?' I asked a very personal question. I felt little bad, thinking that I might have hurt his sentiments.

But he replied with a sad smile, "No. She has always been revered, no one has ever dared to ask any question which may diminish her prestige even after her death. Everyone respects her even today and my friends also know that my love for her was not earthly, but free of any earthly desire."

He stopped there and I could not muster the courage to ask any more questions.

Being a young boy in his early twenties, I could only wonder, how he could sacrifice his youthful days for a lady who had left the world few decades ago, and who had never showed any inclination towards the person who loved her from the core of his heart. In those days, I thought, a lover or a spouse was needed by a person for human needs (physical needs would be a more appropriate phrase perhaps) and of course for emotional support. So frankly speaking, I was not convinced by his philosophy of giving away everything for failed love, just to make it divine in the eyes of others. I thought he was doing injustice to himself and to his parents by sticking to his decision not to marry anyone in his life. However, today at the age of sixty, I understand his love for the lady who refused to love him back, perhaps not because of any shortcomings in him, but for the love for her motherland. Now I am able to understand how one can be happy by giving away everything in lieu of unreciprocated love from a legend of his own time.

Chapter-VIII
Backbiters

In those days, most of the girls were married off by their parents much before the age of sixteen. As Kanaklata grew up to a beautiful young woman, she also got many proposals from many young men. Many proposals came to her father and her stepmother for her hand from eligible bachelors of Barangabari and Gohpur and its adjoining areas. But she always gave one condition, "I shall consider marriage only after India gets her independence."

Unfortunately, she could not see an independent India in her lifetime; but made sure India got her independence through her supreme sacrifice and the supreme sacrifices of many others.

Some respected her decision with humility while some thought she had been arrogant and foolish. However, the second group of people never dared to say anything to her face. Detractors of the Independence movement used to say that she was brainwashed by young leaders like Jyotiprasad Agarwal and Amiyo Kumar Das who happened to be from rich backgrounds, to join the movement so that she could influence the young girls of her age to do the same. Whatever others say, whatever might be the truth, it was a fact that she had influenced hundreds of women of different ages, castes and classes to join the movement for independence of the motherland. In the process she became a headache for the local British administration much before she attained martyrdom.

Even her ardent critics during that period agreed that she grew up to be a beautiful, dusky young woman with great confidence in public speaking. Further, her quick decision-making prowess became the talking point for the general public around Barangabari and its adjoining areas, irrespective of the groups of people who loved her and who criticised her for active participation in the freedom struggle.

Kanaklata Barua was influenced by the youth leaders of Assam during those days like Amiyo Kumar Das and Rup Konwar Jyoti Prasad Aggarwal. However, many critics say she was brainwashed to lead the procession as these leaders knew the danger that would entail those leading the processions at different police stations on that day. To bolster the opinion of the critics, they cited that none of the processions were led by any state level leaders. According to them even local level leaders were not ready to lead the processions and therefore dead and injured did not include any of the leaders nor any of the children of these leaders. The difference between the other leaders and Kanaklata Barua was evident in her selflessness and fearlessness.

Much before September, 1942, the young lady used to meet the leaders at cowsheds owned by another young man of Rampati Rajkhowa whenever the leaders visited Gohpur and other nearby areas. These leaders used the cowsheds as meeting places to contact the local leaders so as to avoid the prying eyes of the spies of the British administration. They were located on the banks of the mighty Brahmaputra, covered with tall grass; a perfect hiding spot for the leaders of the freedom movement. During that period, many stooges of the British government tried to tarnish the image of these leaders and some young female leaders including Kanaklata Barua for their frequent meetings in secluded places. However, as far as Kanaklata Barua was concerned, in most of the meetings, her permanent companion was Hari Hara Rajkhowa who was respected by Kanaklata Barua as a true Gandhian even though she had rejected his proposal for marriage.

When Kanaklata Barua breathed her last, she was a young and a beautiful girl of sweet sixteen or seventeen reportedly, with long hair that reached her knees. She had an adorable smile that invited love and affection from people of all ages. Her poised and helpful nature was a point of discussion in and around her village much before her death on that fateful day.

The backbiters made a U-turn after she attained her martyrdom with grace and poise, and they also started praising her for her selfless and unadulterated love for our motherland.

Chapter-IX
Two Days before the D-Day

18th September, 1942

Among others, Padma Bhushan, Pushpalata Das delivered a fiery speech before a large gathering at the Jaraniyal Satra Namghar urging the masses to join the 'Shanti Bahini' and 'Mrityu Bahini (Death brigade)'. Her speech was so powerful and inspiring, that almost all the common people present in the meeting pledged to join the Mrityu Bahini without a second thought. She urged the people to march to the Gohpur Police station on 20th September, 1942 to hoist the tricolour at the top of the police station symbolising the end of British Raj.

As mentioned in an earlier chapter, Kanaklata had shown great earnestness to join the Mrityu Bahini, even though she was so young. It was this earnestness that allowed her to join it and do something great for her motherland. However, there is a discrepancy in the statement of Pushpalata Das and version of some local persons about her joining the 'Mrityu Bahini'.

According to the local people, she was already a member of the Mrityu Bahini much before Pushpalata Das had met her. Pushpalata Das, after learning of her age, went to Kanaklata's house to tell Kanaklata to withdraw her name from the Mrityu Bahini and the list of participants' names for the September procession.

Kanaklata offered Pushpalata Das a handwoven pictorial chadar, woven by her and offered her tea and *pitha*.

Over a cup of tea, Pushpalata Das asked her, "I heard you have been very active in the organisational works from a tender age. How did you take out time to learn the art of weaving and making pitha?

"Madam, each and every Assamese girl should know weaving and other household chores. Otherwise, how will we be able to serve our motherland after we throw out the British?' Kanaklata replied confidently.

"It is really good thinking from a girl of seventeen. I am sure the whole country will be proud of you one day. But as an older sister, I still advice you to remove your name from the list of Mrityu Bahini and list of participants for the procession to the police station at Gohpur. You can serve the country afterwards as well," Pushpalata Das wanted to convince the young girl, but in vain.

With a sigh of resignation, she looked at the bright face of Kanaklata for some time and then hugged her. Pushpalata could not control her emotions and told her, "Had you been my younger sister or my daughter, I would have locked you up inside a room before joining the procession to the police station, knowing fully well that even then I would have failed to stop you from joining the procession day after tomorrow. I envy your parents. How such a bold girl was blessed to them. I shall not stop you from joining the Mrityu Bahini and the procession seeing your determination. Please take care. God bless you!"

Pushpalata Das got up to leave for her next destination at Kalabari. However, before leaving, she kissed Kanaklata on her forehead, perhaps blessing her to become immortal in the history of the freedom struggle of India.

CHAPTER-X
EARLY MORNING OF THE D-DAY

After getting up early in the morning of that fateful day, Kanaklata hurriedly completed her allotted work of household chores for the day. While doing her chores, she was thinking about an early morning dream of the previous night. In the dream, she had become a fairy and she was taken to fairyland with lot of fanfare by thousands of fairies dressed in beautiful attire. She could not understand why she saw the dream as she had never wanted to be a fairy. It was only the freedom of her motherland that she had always dreamt about. She could not understand whether it was a good dream or a bad dream. On any other day, she would have discussed about the dream with her father or grandfather, but on that day, there was no time. She was in a real hurry to reach the field from where she had to lead the procession to the Gohpur police station.

She ate her *paita bhat* (rice cooked in the previous night kept in a utensil with water) with some salt and chili as quickly as possible. She did not have time to prepare the normal fare for breakfast. Did she have premonition of her death in that morning? Maybe she did.

"*Koli, ajio toi gaa ghelabaloi jabi neki, Bande Mataram chiyariboloi?*" (Koli, are you going out again today to waste your day, chanting Bande Mataram?) Today we have a lot of work in the field. We have to remove the weeds which are covering our paddy," her stepmother called out to her bete-noire Kanaklata. She used her derogatory nick name 'Koli' which means 'black girl' in Assamese.

Her stepmother frowned at her whole hearted involvement in the Independence movement. According to her, any work that required stepping out was meant for the men. For a young girl, doing household chores properly was enough to become a good woman. What added to her fury was that she had to do Kanaklata's share of work as she'd often be away for long hours, participating in agitations and meetings. To be fair to the stepmother, perhaps any biological mother of the 1940s would have reacted in the same manner. (In my book, *My Mother, Dashami Borah,* I have penned down my grandmother's friction with my mother when she used to go to school against my grandmother's wishes.)

However, unlike a normal day, Kanaklata did not react to her stepmother's yelling. Instead, she smiled and said, "You have to remove the weeds all alone from today onwards. I will not be around to hear you scolding me for not doing any household chores or working in the field."

"What is your plan? Are you planning to run away with someone? I mean someone who is also chanting those fancy slogans?" her stepmother taunted.

Had it been another day, Kanaklata would have preferred to fight back. Instead, she replied calmy, "You may be right to some extent. But I am not running away with any mortals, but perhaps with some immortal personalities."

Surprisingly, her stepmother also cooled down and asked, "I cannot understand what you mean. But I understand that you are going for an important noble cause today. Okay, go ahead! I shall do your part of the work. Do not worry. Do you need something more from me now?"

"Yes, I want to wear the gold chain that belonged to my mother. I was told by my father that it was kept for my wedding. Since I am not going to marry anyone till we overthrow the British, I think I should wear the chain today itself, as today may turn out to be a greater day for me than my wedding day," she said smiling sadly.

Her stepmother came out with the gold chain and instinctively put the chain around Kanaklata's neck with all tenderness.

Kanaklata then proceeded to her grandfather's room and asked for his blessings before leaving for the procession. Though it was somewhat unusual of Kanaklata, he blessed her by saying, "I am sure god will help you to do your job well for our motherland."

"Grandpa, I want to hoist the tricolour flag at the top of the Gohpur police station. Bless me so to be strong enough to do that." She wanted a specific blessing from her grandfather.

"I can bless you for your success without any reservation, my child. But I wonder how you will be able to climb the rooftop of the police station!" the old man wondered.

"Grandpa, a bird can fly not because it has two wings but because of having a positive attitude to fly in the sky," Kanaklata replied with a smile.

It was an Assamese proverb where it is said, even without wings one can fly, if the person has a strong will to do so. (Human beings can fly in the sky without wings because of their indomitable spirit.)

"I do not know about the birds, but I know my little granddaughter will be able to do wonders for our motherland. Today, you are known as the granddaughter of Ghanakanta Barua and grandmother, Rohila Barua, and the daughter of Krishnakanta Barua and Karneswari Barua; but who knows from tomorrow whole world will recognise us as the grandparents and parents of a little sweet girl, Kanaklata Barua," the old man thoughtfully said.

"No grandpa, I always want to remain your little granddaughter, Kanaklata. I want to be in your arms whenever I feel sad and rush to the arms of my grandmother whenever I feel the absence of my deceased mother." Kanaklata replied with a sweet smile but sadness in her voice.

"God bless you, my little child. Whatever you want to do, He will be by your side," The old man blessed his granddaughter from his heart with all his love and affection.

The Almighty had already decided the fate of the young girl. He had decided that her ancestors and all the people of her lineage would be known by her name.

She wanted to take blessings from her father as well before leaving home. Unfortunately, her father had already left for their paddy field to evict the unwanted weeds like his young daughter who wanted throw away the British flag fluttering at the top of the police station of Gohpur.

She met her younger brothers and sisters and told them with unusual calmness to study properly and follow the advice of the elders. Her younger siblings were surprised as that was the first time she had spoken to them in such a manner before leaving home for attending some socio-political duties. Perhaps that morning, her subconscious mind was having overwhelming effects on her behaviour.

Her stepmother waved goodbye to her, much to her surprise. Kanaklata found the behaviour of her stepmother unusual. She felt happy, hoping for a better relation with her stepmother and smiled back at her.

She ran to the Jaraniyal Satra Namghar as she was already late by a few minutes.

Chapter-XI
The Procession

The people had started gathering at Jaraniyal Satra Namghar from early morning of 20th September, 1942 to march to the Gohpur police station. They aimed to hoist the flag to mark the symbolical end of British Raj in India, for the time being. Everyone was eager to go the police station without delay as they did not want to be the last ones to be at the police station. However, the village elders thought otherwise.

They advised all the volunteers to take part in a short prayer meeting before proceeding to Gohpur police station in a procession as per scheduled programme. All the people present there requested them to conduct the prayer meeting and keep it as short as possible as the distance they had to cover on foot was thirteen kilometres. This meant they would take at least four hours to cover the distance. The elders obliged their request, considering the importance and urgency of the matter.

The prayer was organised and blessings from the almighty were sought for their safe and successful return from Gohpur by uttering the final chanting, *'Owaa Hari, owaa Ram. Owaa Ram. Owaa Hari.'*

All the people present there felt that they were protected by the almighty on that day and were ready to face any eventuality.

Unfortunately, the destined girl arrived a little too late to take the blessings of the prayer meeting. Perhaps, the almighty had given her the ultimate blessing from Him, to become immortal in the history of the freedom movement and make the people of Assam indebted to her for all the time to come.

Seeing her running to the prayer hall, an elderly villager asked her, "Did you face the same problem leaving your home to serve the motherland like any other day?"

He knew how her stepmother used to be angry every time she would leave the house.

'No uncle, today my mother was very considerate. See, I am wearing a gold chain. Believe it or not, she not only gave it to me, but helped me to wear it as well," with a sweet smile, the teenager replied.

"Oh, so today you have been blessed by your mother also. I am sure today you are going to do something special, which will not only make your family proud, but also our entire area," the old man said with a broad smile.

"Yes, koka, bless me so that I can make my family proud along with the entire people of Barangabari and Gohpur," she said with another sweet smile.

She thought for a second and then said, "Why only Barangabari and Gohpur? Why not entire Assam or the entire country?"

"I am sure one day the whole country will be proud of you, my child. God bless you." The elderly man kissed the head of the teenager, oblivious of the fact that his blessing would be realised within a few hours of their meeting.

The young girl with long hair touched the feet of the old man. The elderly man wanted to say something more, but before he could say something, a friend of Kanaklata, Navami took her away. Another girl, Sewali, apologised to the elderly person, "Sorry, grandpa, we are already late and we have to gather the people for our procession."

"No problem, my child. I understand the importance and paucity of time for the most important event. Go ahead, my blessings are with all of you," the elderly man blessed them once again.

Navami, Kanaklata's friend whispered, "Kanaklata, Hari Hara *kakaideo* is looking for you."

With a mischievous twinkle in her eyes, Navami teased Kanaklata, "Why don't you say yes to his proposal? He loves you very much. He can die for you."

"But I cannot die for anyone except for the motherland. I cannot love anyone till India gets her independence. Anyway, where is he?" Kanaklata snubbed her.

Hari Hara was waiting for Kanaklata eagerly. As soon as he saw her, he told, "Kanaklata, everyone present here wants you to lead the procession. I also want you to. In fact, you deserve to lead the procession for your love for our motherland and for your contribution to the Independence movement. But if you see some danger, please let me face it first," he requested Kanaklata, knowing fully well that she would never do that.

As expected, she replied, "What you have mentioned as danger, I think will be an opportunity for me to serve my country better. However, I shall be grateful to you for your concern for me," she told Hari Hara politely.

Hari Hara did not say anything; he only nodded.

After talking to Hari Hara, Kanaklata talked about her early morning dream to her close friend Navami. Navami immediately retorted, "Today you are going to meet your prince charming."

"I am not interested in meeting any prince charming. If I get someone, I shall pass him on to you. Happy?" Kanaklata replied with her trademark smile. Both the friends started laughing.

After fifteen minutes, the march began, with Kanaklata leading the procession to Gohpur police station, chanting the popular slogans, 'Vande Mataram' and 'Bharat chhodo."

The people behind her did not have an inkling that they were following a legend for all time to come. None perhaps thought, all of them were going to witness a historical event from a very close range, and were also going to be a part of the history of Assam. They were ignorant that in the history of the freedom struggle of India, a chapter would be devoted for their sacrifice and valour in that morning. Navami, Sewali and Kanaklata's other friends never thought they were going to lose their most charismatic friend forever. The acquaintances never had any idea that they were not going to see the beautiful smile in their life once again. They never thought the young lady with long thick hair would be consigned to flames that evening in the presence of thousands of people.

The procession was moving slowly but very steadily. As it moved towards Gohpur, it swelled into a sea of people comprising of teenaged youngsters to octogenarian grandfathers. The number of males was equally matched by females from different age groups. The procession was filled with people from all classes and all castes, from all religions and all walks of life, including the 'chah mazdoors' of the adjoining tea gardens.

It was happening at the same time all over India; a number of processions were moving towards the local police stations with a large number of people from all walks of life. All the processions had only one aim – to remove the British flag fluttering at the top of the police station and replacing it with a tricolour.

That day, British power in India was going to get a taste of 'people's power' in India.

Chapter-XII
Police Preparation

A few days before the D-Day, the entry points of the police station were barricaded by bamboo poles so that the protesters would not be able to enter the police station directly. The officer in charge, Officer Gom ordered the police constables to check their rifles daily and advised to them to practice target shooting for the past one week prior to 20th September, 1942. It is said that at that time the Gohpur police station was not a large police station and was manned by only a few constables. Therefore, all the constables were asked to report for their duties at 6 a.m. on that day without any deviation. Those who were on leave on that day were also asked to report for duty. He warned, if any of the constables would fail to come that morning, the absentee constable would be arrested for treason against the British Empire. The absentee constable would not only be arrested, but was likely to be declared as an absconder and his properties would be confiscated by the government.

All the policemen reached the police station much before the scheduled reporting time that day, fearing disciplinary action against them. The policemen were well aware of the fact that the British administration could be ruthless against those who dared to go against them; particularly by any government servant. Policemen were more vulnerable compared to other government servants as far as punishment for neglecting their assigned duties were concerned. Again, the Indian British policemen were the most hated persons in those days for their role against the freedom struggle. In a sense, they were caught in a catch 22 situation.

The policemen might have also prayed to the Almighty hoping no untoward incident would take place in their police station. After all, all the policemen were Indians, obliged to perform their duties against their personal will. Who knows, some of their own relatives were also taking part in the freedom struggle in some other areas? Who knows, some of their relatives were also expected to join the procession at Gohpur itself? All the policemen were tense since early morning.

The officer in charge of Gohpur police station addressed the police constables posted under his command in the early morning of 20th September, 1942 with a brave face, though he was extremely tense.

"My dear friends, as I told you yesterday, today will be our testing time to prove ourselves as brave British government servants. Yesterday, I was expecting some reinforcement from other police stations or from the district police headquarters to tackle the problem of facing thousands of people coming from four sides of our police station. But probably, all the police stations are facing shortage of manpower. The lathi-wielding (baton wielding) battalion has been deployed at Bihali Police station as the authority thinks the number of protesters in that area may be less and can be controlled by lathi. Since we have lesser number of policemen and may have to tackle more people, we cannot take a 'second chance'. So please do not carry any lathi to burden yourself; carry the gun with maximum ammunition with you when you are facing the protesters today. Give only one verbal warning to disperse and the next warning should be a blank fire and third warning should be a shot on the chest of the protester who will be leading the procession."

A young constable dared to ask a question, "Sir, if the procession is led by a big leader, please let us know whether we should shoot him or her?"

"It is a pertinent question, which I must answer. As per our information, most of the top leaders are already in jail. Even many second rung leaders have also already been arrested. However, there are still some leaders at large who have been able to escape arrest till today. They are unlikely to lead a protest fearing possible arrest. Even then if you see some influential leaders at the front lines, arrest them, and then open fire. Is it clear? Any doubt?"

He did not want to take the risk of killing a leader without specific instruction from his boss sitting at Tezpur, the district HQs.

Then he said thoughtfully, "I have information that one female leader is instigating the people to join the procession in large numbers in the Gohpur area and in Dhekiajuli. The administration is anticipating more trouble in these areas. That is really bad news for all of us."

The same constable who raised a question earlier raised another question, "Can we expect her at our police station?"

"So far as I know, she is not leading any procession. But that will not ease our problem. A young firebrand girl from

Barangabari is leading one of the four processions," Officer Gom told the policemen.

"I know her; she must be Kanaklata Barua. My wife is from Barangabari. She is extremely bold and dedicated. At the same time, she is very calm and polite," a policeman informed.

"I have information about her. But she is not a very big leader in the eyes of our bosses sitting at Tezpur and Shillong. But still, we should tackle her appropriately as she is from the most influential family of Barangabari. Try to avoid firing at her, unless you think that is unavoidable," Officer Gom did not elaborate what he had meant by saying 'tackle appropriately'. Then he asked his policemen, "Any doubt?"

"No, sir!" All the constables uttered in unison.

"Constable Boro and Constable Gohain, I find that you both are very brave. Therefore, both of you have to stand in the first line. Even if, after firing by both of you, the protesters do not disperse, the second line will fire at the protesters. So, in the second line, Constable Sharma, Constable Saikia and Constable Borah will take over from Constable Gohain and Constable Boro. I shall order you when to fire. Any question? Any doubt?"

"No, sir." Again, all the constables uttered in unison.

(*Names of the constables and the concerned police officers have been changed.*)

Chapter-XIII
Second Bullet

When the procession led by Kanaklata Barua reached the periphery of the Gohpur police station, they saw that the protesters from Kalabari-side and Lohitmukh-side had already arrived. After a short discussion among the local leaders of Barangabari, Gohpur, Lohitmukh and Kalabari, it was decided that the western side of the gate will be approached by protesters from Barangabari, led by Kanaklata Barua.

When the protesters of Barangabari reached the western gate of the Gohpur police station, her procession was warned not to advance further by Constable Boro.

Kanaklata Barua replied with the usual calmness in her voice, "We are peaceful protesters. Why do you want to stop us?"

"I do not know why you have come here, but I know one thing, if you do not disperse from here, I have an order from my boss to fire upon you. I am a government servant who has to obey the order of the boss, not to ask him why. So please go away, otherwise I will be compelled to fire!" Constable Boro thundered.

"You are bound by the order of your boss. But I am driven by a passion; a passion of deep love for my country. You people are bought by the British government with a few pennies. We are not bought by anyone. But if you have little love for our motherland, please step aside and let us go inside and help us in hoisting the flag. In any case, you have to hoist our flags at the top of the police station after a few days, or after a few months or in the worst case, after a few years. It is just a matter of time," Kanaklata tried to convince the policeman, standing before her, aiming his 303-rifle pointing at her chest.

"I have tolerated your nonsense for a pretty long time only because you are a young girl of my sister's age, otherwise, if you were an adult male, I would have fired long back!" Constable Boro thundered again.

"Do not distinguish between a male and a female who is a member of the Mrityu Bahini. We have already pledged to die for our motherland without committing any violent activities. Vande Mataram!" Kanaklata replied without fear, but a lot of pride.

"I shall not hesitate to fire at you if you do not leave the place right now," the policeman with the gun once again thundered.

"I am already in fire; the fire ignited by the patriotism that lives inside me. When there is fire inside a heart, nobody can understand how much heat it can generate and how devastating it can be. I am not fearful of death. You can kill me but you cannot kill my spirit of patriotism." Kanaklata replied without any fear in her voice.

"Don't you feel for your parents? What will happen if you lose your life today?' He took a different route to persuade the young lady with beautiful long bouncy black hair to disperse from the western gate of the Gohpur police station.

"If I die today, not only my parents, but also the entire

locality will be proud of me. On the other hand, if you kill me, you will be remorseful after some time. Your family will also abandon you. None of your relatives will take your name with pride. Rather they will be ashamed of taking your name in front of others," Kanaklata gave a different dimension to their argument.

"I know, you are from a good family but brainwashed by the leaders who have never sent their own children for a procession where there is a chance of facing bullets or facing the deadly blows of the lathis of the policemen," he made a jab on the leaders of the unsuspecting common freedom fighters.

"No one has brainwashed me. But yes, my inner feeling has been ignited by the speeches of the patriot leaders. They taught me about patriotism in minute details. I am here on my own will knowing fully well what may happen to me in the worst-case scenario," she countered.

"I heard that a lady had visited different places under our police station to instigate people. But today she is nowhere to be seen," the constable referred to a leader.

"Do not say anything bad about her. She is a revered lady. Have you lost your senses while speaking about a respected lady?" This time Kanaklata grew agitated.

Before the constable could reply to her counter argument, there was a push from behind. The cumulative effect of the push pushed Kanaklata towards Constable Boro.

Without finding out the real reason of the push of the crowd, he perhaps thought Kanaklata was moving towards him aggressively because of the comment he had made on the lady leader. He perhaps forgot the advice of Inspector Gom to make a blank fire to disperse the crowd before firing at the chest of the leader. Therefore, without issuing the mandatory blank fire warning before firing at the protestors, and without waiting for the order of the boss to fire upon the protesters, Constable Boro fired upon Kanaklata.

The bold young lady of sweet sixteen collapsed immediately uttering the following words, "Vande Mataram, Jai Bharat, Jai Ai Asom."

Hari Hara Rajkhowa who was a few steps behind Kanaklata, tried to pull her away from the line of fire, so that the second bullet wouldn't hit her. He was successful in doing so, but the bullet grazed along his head. Blood started flowing from his head profusely. He did not care for his life; he tried to save her and lifted her from the ground. He tried to run to a safer place with the senseless body of Kanaklata on his shoulder. Later on, the third bullet perhaps killed Mukunda Kakati who had picked up the tricolour from the hands of Kanaklata Barua.

The fact was that there was no one there to record the mayhem caused by the British police that morning. Many claim only two bullets were fired; the official version might have also confirmed that claim. Like Hari Hara, many were injured by the bullets of the British police at the Gohpur police station; but none could go to the government hospital for proper treatment fearing further atrocities in the hands of the rogue policemen. There was no dearth of British stooges within the masses expecting some favours from them. Therefore, those injured with bullets, remained untreated and remained unknown entities even after India got her independence, five years later.

It may be true not only for the Gohpur police firing incident but also true for many other similar incidents that took place throughout India. In Assam at the Dhekiajuli police station, at least eleven patriots belonging to modest backgrounds were killed in police firing, while scores were injured. Unfortunately, these martyrs remained unknown.

A pertinent question may disturb your minds, 'Why were the names of those people who succumbed to the bullet injuries or the brutal lathi charges due to lack of proper medical treatment, not retrieved in the post-independence era?'

There might be many reasons. I have requested the historians and research scholars, in general and of Assam in particular, to find answers of my queries in a different chapter – 'Food for thought'.

Returning to that morning, Hari Hara Rajkhowa tried to carry Kanaklata to a safer place assuming that she would survive the bullet injury. He did not know that his efforts to save Kanaklata would go in vain as she had left the world forever much before Hari Hara had lifted her from the ground. He did not know how long he was running and in which direction. After a while, he also lost consciousness due to the heavy bleeding from his temple. He could not remember what happened afterwards.

When he regained his consciousness, he found himself in the lap of an old lady who was putting a bandage on his head. He could not recall why he was lying there and how long he had been there. He could not understand why a bandage was wrapped around his head.

However, a few seconds later, he was able to identify the lady. She was Sarala aunty who had been working as a midwife in the Gohpur Government Dispensary for many years before she was fired from her service on the suspicion of having close relations with the freedom fighters. Slowly, he was able to recall everything that had taken place.

The first question Hari Hara asked Sarala aunty, "Where is Kanaklata? Is she okay?"

"Kanaklata has been taken away by her parents in an injured state. I do not know how is she right now." Sarala aunty was aware of the fact that Kanaklata had already passed away, but she knew the injured Hari Hara was in no state to receive the news.

"Aunty, I know she will be alright. She loves the country more than anyone of us. God will help her to serve the country better in future. God bless her," he said before closing his eyes once again because of the weakness due to excessive bleeding.

However, when he came to learn that Kanaklata was no more in this world the next day, he was shattered.

He told Sarala aunty, "She will be living in the hearts of millions of people of our country. She and her spirit will never die, as long as Assam and India live. I am happy I could carry her on my shoulders for some time. God had been kind enough to me to give that opportunity. If she had been alive even for a second on my shoulders, I am the happiest man in the world. I shall pray to the almighty to give me a second chance to carry her on my shoulders when she will sacrifice her life once again for our motherland for another sacred cause."

Hari Hara had never cried over the death of Kanaklata; but he was always proud that he was able to carry her for some time and had saved her from the second bullet which hit his temple.

When he narrated the story about the supreme sacrifice of Kanaklata Barua, I could see only pride in his eyes; no remorse and no sadness.

"Do you have any regrets, Grandpa?" I asked him softly.

"Yes, only one regret," he told me after a deep thought.

"What was that?" I asked.

"If instead of picking up Kanaklata, had I picked up the flag, I would have been killed by the policeman along with her. Probably, I loved Kanaklata more than the motherland. On the other hand, Mukunda Kakati, like Kanaklata, loved the country more than anything else. That is why, both Kanaklata and Mukunda Kakati are martyrs and I am going to die one day as an obscure ordinary man." This time he wiped his moist eyes.

Though I was very young, I could understand that his regret was genuine. After few years, I heard an English veteran of World War II, who said on record that he was extremely unhappy as a survivor of World War II because none cares for any war survivor, but everyone respects a soldier who laid down his life for his country.

Yes, we always will respect Kanaklata Barua, the martyr, more than any freedom fighter, even if, he or she went on to become a minister or was able to hold a very high post.

Chapter-XIV
Vidyadhar Lahon

Like many patriots from modest backgrounds in Dhekiajuli, at least one patriot of Gohpur from a poor background also reportedly succumbed to a bullet injury after few months of the firing. Unfortunately, the martyrs who did not die instantly did not get any publicity in both the British period and after India became an independent country. Similarly, the injured patriots also did not get any publicity so they are not known to the present generation of people even within their own localities.

Vidyadhar Lahon (name changed) was also one of the young men who sacrificed his life. He died due to a bullet injury at the hands of the policemen posted at Gohpur police station that morning. As mentioned, he was also one of the unlucky martyrs who did not die instantly; his martyrdom is unheard of and remains unwritten in the history books of Assam till today.

According to the local people of Gohpur, Vidyadhar was a poor young boy of thirteen, the only son of a young widow, but full of patriotism. He lost his life after six months of the tragic incident. He was also hit by a bullet on his arm that fateful morning of 20th September, 1942 behind the Gohpur police station.

According to the elderly citizens of Gohpur, the young boy tried to hoist the flag scaling the wall of the police station from the back. However, as he was climbing the wall, he was seen by a policeman who fired upon the young boy without showing any mercy even though he was a mere teenaged boy. Fortunately, (or unfortunately) the bullet missed the head or chest of the boy; but hit his arm, and he missed the glory of martyrdom.

Being a very young boy, he lost his mental balance due to the trauma of almost being killed by a bullet. In those days there was no counselling facility for a traumatised person. Further, due to unattended bullet injury, his injury aggravated slowly and steadily. Ultimately, after six months, away from public eyes, he lost his life without any glory.

Few elderly persons still recall him and confide with some others about his supreme sacrifice for the motherland. But these types of discussions are limited to few persons and that too in private conversations only. Unfortunately, nobody wants to document the sacrifices of that teenaged boy and others who also reportedly died due to bullet injury or due to lack of proper medical treatments. During British rule, due to fear of retaliation by the British government, the poor and non-influential effected families did not dare to talk of these martyrs in public. After independence, perhaps, these poor families want to open up their hearts about the supreme sacrifices of their near and dear ones. However, might be due to jealousy on the part of the neighbours or due to some unknown selfish reasons of some leaders of the past and present generation, sacrifices of these martyrs have been blacked out even today.

A group of local people doubt, that if Vidyadhar Lahon gets the recognition of scaling the walls of the Gohpur police station in the morning of 20th September, 1942, but not making the supreme sacrifice on that day for the motherland, he may lose some importance in the history books and in the society. This particular group of local people blames those influential people in the society for not honouring the supreme sacrifice of that particular boy under reference. This group of people even blames some of the top leaders and freedom fighters of Assam during that period for the unfortunate goof up. According to them if the heroics of the boy are recorded, the history of Assam may have to be rewritten (at least for the Gohpur police firing incident).

Without taking any side, either of the documented history and the hearsay on the incident, I sincerely hope the truth will prevail one day.

Again, I am reiterating, I do not know whether the unknown boy actually made the supreme sacrifice or not on that particular day, but if he did, I sincerely hope that the unknown boy will also be honoured by the people of modern Assam as an unsung hero of the India's struggle for independence and he will also be remembered alongside the other martyrs of Assam.

However, in my personal opinion, Kanaklata had some unparalleled qualities of bravery, leadership, public speaking, story-telling capacity, showing utmost calmness in worst possible situations apart from her helpful attitude towards one and all.

Chapter-XV
The Aftermath

The body of Kanaklata Barua was carried by the patriotic people of Barangabari along village roads avoiding the main road, fearing that the British administration might prevent an honourable cremation of the martyr by the people. The freedom fighters also did not want her body to be sent for post mortem where the dignity of a lady would be the first casualty. Her body was hidden from the spies of the British administration till she was consigned to the flames that evening in the presence of thousands of patriotic people of Barangabari, Gohpur, Kalabari and people from other far-flung areas of Darrang district.

Kanaklata's death actually gave birth to a legend to be worshipped. That evening, everyone present there wanted to see her face for the last time before she was laid down on the *chita* (pyre). From children to elderly people, they all carried flowers, colourful *japis* (a kind of traditional head gear to honour someone) and *gamochas* to place on her dead body. The offerings created a mound on the body of the young heroic girl.

The old lady who was nursed by Kanaklata few years ago lamented, "How brutal can the British administration be to kill a girl with such a sweet smile? How can one kill such a helpful young lady so ruthlessly?"

Many echoed her sentiments. Many spoke about her bravery, many of her eloquent public speaking, and many spoke about her calmness at the time of provocation. They spoke about her helpful nature and about her talent to weave dreams on a gamocha or on a chadar, and about her contribution to girls' education. During her cremation, everybody recalled her one or more of the special qualities of the young brave heart, as they prayed for the departed soul to rest in peace.

The mourners were sure that only the dead body of Kanaklata was consigned to flames that day; not her spirit and love for our motherland. They also realised that lifeless Kanaklata was much more powerful than Kanaklata herself when she had been alive.

When finally, her father lit the pyre, people shouted at the top of their voices,

"Kanaklata amar howk!" (Kanaklata will be immortal)

British police, go to hell!

Vande Mataram! Bharat Mataki jai!

Jai Ai Asom! Murderer Britishers go back home!'

The thunderous chanting of the people perhaps sent a chilling shock wave through the spine of the administration.

Her death caused a ripple effect in the British administration. It is said, the opposition party of Great Britain raised a question in the British Parliament about the firing at an unarmed young girl from point-blank range. The opposition also voiced their opinion against the oppressive policy of the ruling party.

In the meantime, pressure was mounting on the British government by the US led countries of the allied forces for the freedom of India. One should remember the precondition of US in joining the allied force was: restoring of democracy and freedom of speech of the common people of the entire world, freedom from political hegemony of one or few countries over the other countries and so on. Therefore, after the formation of the UN at the end of World War II, the freedom of India from British rule was a foregone conclusion.

In fact, the independence of India was the culmination of three major factors: mass participation in the Independence movement by the common people of India, the US joining the allied forces with the precondition of giving freedom to the colonies from the European powers and loss of Hitler in the World War-II. Since the order of influence is debatable, I prefer to say, the order of influence of these factors without any particular order. However, if we go by the popular sentiment of the people of India, I have to go by the order I have mentioned above.

At the local level, Constable Boro lost his mind for killing an innocent girl without any provocation on her part. Even his colleague who was standing with a gun, Gohain, criticised Boro for firing upon Kanaklata that morning. His boss also washed his hands off the killing of Kanaklata Barua and Mukunda Kakati by saying that he had never uttered the word 'fire' from his mouth. Constable Boro had opened fire on the protesters, particularly on Kanaklata Barua that morning on his own.

Other policemen may have also fired upon the protesters. Since nobody had died in front of the police station, government hushed up the actual number of rounds fired and the involvement of other constables. Thus, the official records might have mentioned that only two rounds of firing had taken place that morning and only Constable Boro was involved. The preliminary enquiry and subsequent report prepared by the British categorically blamed only Constable Boro who had fired two rounds from his 303-rifle. Most of the historians of Assam also blamed only him for the killing of Kanaklata Barua and Mukunda Kakati that bloody morning. Thus, instead of getting support and appreciation from the colleagues and his boss for following the order of the boss without any deviation, he was castigated by all. Many people, particularly Assamese historians marked his character as a trigger-happy police constable of the British administration.

After six months of the incident, the body of Constable Boro was recovered from a well. His death was recorded as a suicide case; but nobody knows whether it was indeed a suicide case or a case of murder to mislead the expected enquiry at the behest of the opposition party of the British Parliament about the killing of the innocent teenaged girl. Had he been alive, many things would have surfaced; how many constables were actually involved in the firing incident? How many rounds of firing had taken place? Whether Inspector Gom had actually uttered the word, 'fire' before Constable Boro fired his first shot or not, and so on. No one in the police administration wanted to open the Pandora's box which might have tarnished the image of British administration. Is this the reason of death of Constable Boro? Because a dead man cannot defend himself if all the blame is attributed to him? I cannot say anything for sure; but I know many sham judicial enquiries had been undertaken and many sham judgements were passed during the British rule in India against our brave-hearts to safeguard their interests.

When she was alive, she might have been a bold, helpful girl living next door. After her untimely and unfortunate death, she became an enigma for her supporters and for the British administration as well. The sound of her silence reached the corridors of the British Parliament. Lifeless Kanaklata was a thousand times more powerful communicator and an inspiring leader than the living young girl of seventeen. Kanaklata Barua's ability to inspire people after her martyrdom had jumped many folds during the freedom struggle of India.

What was surprising was that, for killing eleven persons at the Dhekiajuli police station, there was no political storm neither at the British Parliament nor at the local level. So far, I know, none of the constables who had killed so many persons and injured hundreds of patriots faced enquiry and alienation from their own policemen. As far as I know, none of the policemen of Dhekiajuli police station had committed suicide, nor anyone went into a state of depression. In 1976, I learnt about the involvement of a person I know in the killing of the protestors in front of the Dhekiajuli police station.

I was told the 'uncle' had been cursed by the mother of the martyr by saying, "You could have fired at the legs of my son instead of firing at his chest. One day, you will also get the same punishment at the hands of the Almighty."

It is hard to say, whether because of the curse or otherwise, the police constable (by the time he had changed his job and was living a jolly good personal and public life) lost his own son in a road accident in 1976.

The people of the area reacted to the personal tragedy saying that it was the curse of the bereaved lady who had lost her young son in the firing incident at the Dhekiajuli police station on 20th September, 1942. Many opined that the soul of the young martyr came to life as a son, just to take revenge on him. I do not know how many people will believe that story of revenge, but we perhaps cannot avoid the fallout of our own karma in this life or beyond.

After India got her independence, Kanaklata Barua got the status of a demigoddess, but the police officials who took part directly or indirectly in those gruesome killing of the patriots lived a life of solitude as outcasts. I must admit though, everyone involved may not have faced the same treatment from the society, thanks to the public opinion built up because of specific reasons or otherwise, just like all the brave-hearts did not get equal status or publicity even after Independence.

Many institutions, stadiums, memorials are named after Kanaklata Barua. Even an INS has been named after Kanaklata Barua by the Indian Navy, remembering her supreme sacrifice on the morning of 20th September, 1942. My book too is a small tribute to the great lady along with the lesser-known martyrs of the freedom struggle of India, who made supreme sacrifices for the country.

However, I was surprised and shocked to hear of an incident of a few petty influential people of a particular organisation (Barangabari Unit) during my recent visit to Barangabari and Gohpur. The statue of Kanaklata Barua erected in front of Gohpur Police station, which I have also seen many times from my childhood days, had been brought to Barangabari, instead of erecting a larger statue at Barangabari by the people of

Barangabari. However, I restrain any further comment as I do not want to stoke controversy on a sensitive issue.

Though she was a young girl, Kanaklata's mentors were renowned people. Her mentor, Pushpalata Das went on to become the first lady MP of Assam and got her Padma Bhushan award from the Government of India for her contribution to the freedom struggle of India. Her literary contributions have also been recognised by the Assamese people across generations.

One of her mentors, Jyotiprasad Agarwala was also an icon of Assam and he was bestowed the honour of 'Rup Konwar' of Assam. Incidentally, he made the first Assamese film, *Jaymati* much before India attained her independence. It is said, his play, *Labhita* was inspired by the life of Kanaklata Barua, though that is debatable. Many people claim that Kanaklata Barua's publicity increased because of the play which I don't believe to be true, nor do I think it is false propaganda made against her supreme sacrifice. However, I do believe that other martyrs of Assam should get publicity so that we, the Assamese people also can boast about the martyrdom of patriots from rural Assam.

Another mentor, Amiyo Kumar Das, popularly addressed as Lok Nayak, went on to become a cabinet minister of Assam with different portfolios such as Education, Labour and Food and Civil Supplies, during various periods till his death in 1975. He translated the book *My Experiments with Truth,* the autobiography of Mahatma Gandhi, into Assamese. He was also awarded the Padma Bhushan in 1963 for his contributions to the Indian freedom struggle and for his social work. He married Pushpalata Das and they had one daughter.

CHAPTER-XVI
LAST DAYS OF HARI HARA RAJKHOWA

I can live without you,
But I cannot live without the memory of you.
I know,
I am unable to say
A good morning to you,
In the early morning of a day,
Or
I am unable to say
A good afternoon to you,
In the afternoon of a day.
Neither,
I am able to say
A good night to you,
Before going to bed
Nor
I am able to say
Sweet dreams to you,
On every evening,
As I wished to say.

But,
I am able to wish silently and surely,
Be happy as always,
Wherever you are,
After the day of supreme sacrifice by you,
For our motherland,
By taking a barrage of bullets,
On your chest,
But not on your back.

***

Hari Hara Rajkhowa may have lived a soul-less life as rendered in the verse after the death of Kanaklata.

A bachelor lives like a king and dies like a dog, says an old proverb. However, it was not so. Hari Hara Rajkhowa was no ordinary bachelor. After his retirement from the government job in the early seventies till his last day in the later part of eighties, he was actively involved in social work. He did not suffer from any major ailment in his entire life and therefore, he did not take sick leave even for a single day.

He died of a massive heart attack in 1987 at the age of seventy when I was posted at Giridih. Though he was physically fit, he might have had a premonition of his death few days prior to his demise according to some of his relatives. A few days prior to his death, he told his nephew that if he were to die shortly, he should be consigned to flames as close as possible to the cremation ground where the martyr was cremated.

I do not know whether his last wish could be fulfilled or not by his family members. However, in my opinion, his soul must have been very happy to leave this world to be reunited with the girl with long beautiful hair.

I feel an immense sense of sadness for Hari Hara koka for two reasons – had the 'missed bullet' hit him one inch deeper, he would have also made supreme sacrifice for our country and his name would also have been taken alongwith the legend, Kanaklata Barua. Secondly, despite having sacrificed his entire life for his one-sided love affair for a lady who could not reciprocate his love because of her love for her country was overwhelming, compared to her personal choice and comfort, he did not get any praise from the society at large. He went through life alone. And he left this world with an obscure final good bye like an ordinary man, despite giving his life for society in a way.

Perhaps, for all the people around him, he had been an ordinary man, but for me. He was also a hero, with unparallel qualities of an extraordinary selfless man with a large heart, who kept aside his personal loss to serve the society.

CHAPTER-XVII
FOOD FOR THOUGHT

I am posing a few relevant questions to history students and research scholars. This is food for thought on the history of Assam, an attempt to question and discuss history as documented and the history that was left untold:

1. Why did the martyrs of Dhekiajuli not get any importance in the history books of Assam like the ones of Gohpur and Barhampur?
2. When the name of the constable who killed Kanaklata Barua was widely publicised, why did the names of the policemen involved in the massacre of Dhekiajuli not given equal publicity?
3. Was there a sinister design for these select omissions and commissions?
4. Why couldn't all the names of the martyrs of Patharughat and Phulaguri be retrieved even by the historians of independent India?
5. Why were the supreme sacrifices of the tea garden workers recorded as mere skirmishes between management and labourers, when the management of these tea gardens were mostly represented by the Britishers in the pre-independence era?

6. Why, so far in Assam, none of the tribal martyrs or any of the martyrs from tea garden community have been idolised?
7. Is there any chance of re-writing our history books at least for the period since 1826?
8. Why was police brutality perpetrated only in two police stations on 20th September, 1942? Incidentally, both the police stations were separated by only 140 kilometres. Is there any connection between these two police stations? Or, is there any connection between the leaders spearheading the Independence movement in these two places?
9. Is there a role of any particular leader in these areas which led to the volatile situations which culminated in the death of more than ten people in front of the two police stations?
10. So far as Bhogeswari Phukanani is concerned, an account of her bravery has been recorded. But the bravery of the other martyrs remains unknown. Why?
11. During any agitation, the agitators are usually the first to provoke, though the organisers of the agitations never admit that fact for obvious reasons. Was that the case in the Gohpur and Dhekiajuli conflicts between the police force and the agitators? Or was it otherwise?
12. If the above point is true, why did the agitators behave in such a fashion when in most of the police stations of Assam, the tricolour flags were hoisted without loss of any human life?

13. Is there any leader of the Congress party who instigated the common masses to indulge in violence from a safe distance?
14. If the answer to the above point is yes, then who was he or she?
15. If point no.11, 12 and 13 have affirmative answers, then has that leader received any benefits after independence in terms of award, money and position?

Annexure I

An Incomplete List of Martyrs of Assam

01. Piyali Barphukan
02. Jiuram Barua
03. Maniram Dewan
04. Piyali Barua
05. Kushal Konwar
06. Kanaklata Barua
07. Maniram Kachari
08. Hemoram Pator
09. Gunabhi Bordoloi
10. Lerela Boro
11. Ratan Kachari
12. Lakhi Hazarika
13. Thagi Sut
14. Boloram Sut
15. Madan Barman,
16. Rauta Boro
17. Nidhanu Rajbangshi
18. Mungri alias Malati Mem
19. Dariki Dasi Baruah
20. Rebati Lahon
21. Khahuli Devi
22. Tileswari Barua
23. Kumali Devi
24. Padumi Gogoi
25. Thunuki Das
26. Jaluki Kachariani
27. Kon Chutiani
28. Lila Neogoni
29. Lakshman Singh Deka
30. Sangbar Lalung
31. Rangbar Deka
32. Manbar Nath
33. Kumali Devi
34. Mohiram Koch

35. Tileswari Baruah
36. Moniram Kochari
37. Ratan Kochari
38. Aruna Chutiya
39. Dayal Manika
40. Mangal Kurku
41. Chandan Sharma
42. Dharma Panda
43. Datu Suri
44. Pradeep Rai
45. Pator Roop
46. Layan Koch
47. Ranga Suleg
48. Manik Deka
49. Bhaneswar Doley
50. Kamala
51. Hatrala Mandal
52. Usha Mandal
53. Joy Dhan
54. Hari Deka
55. Chura Moni Deka
56. Bihu Ram Saloi
57. Kali Rai
58. Rangmon Mena
59. Bora Mena
60. Hadiram
61. Ranjit Saloi
62. Dhoni
63. Rukum Khura
64. Mehiram
65. Haudya
66. Kinaram
67. Sambu Koch
68. Two person from a marriage party
69. One Begger
70. Bokul Koch
71. Dhanjay Kalia
72. Torog Deka
73. Bhadya Keot
74. Dilo Koch
75. Hojil Sheikh
76. Alin Sheikh
77. Behba Sheikh
78. Thoga Bhoria Sheikh
79. Sanjay (Kalia) Kalita
80. Hoba Ram Bhordoli
81. Aogon Mera Kait
82. Tuni Koch
83. Baiut Kait
84. Muno Horma
85. Kina Ram
86. Dhumo Horman
87. Pranoy Hori Horma
88. Bhor likhi Sheikh

89. Kata Sheikh
90. Ghon Diyo Sheikh
91. Bholi Sheikh
92. Bhokol Koch
93. Bhaguru Koch
94. Hile Kuchiya Bhura
95. Atiya Koch
96. Shishu Ram Koch
97. Loyen Koch
98. Ranga Saloi
99. Jhuron Koch
100. Sharu Babubez
101. Ratimol
102. Holiram
103. Tamdon Deka
104. Bhati Rai Gahora
105. Modhuri Koch
106. Chuwabor Lalung
107. Thomba Lalung,
108. Moira Singh,
109. Leleu,
110. Bhedeu,
111. Nal Dom,
112. Lahar Nath,
113. Beer Singh,
114. Hafiz Miya
115. Christison Munda
116. Doyal Das Panika
117. Mongol Kurku
118. Tehlu Saora
119. Bankuru Saora

At the Patharughat Martyr Memorial, a statement has been written in Assamese that the list of Martyrs is incomplete. According to the memorial inscription 71 names are available out of 141 martyrs who laid down their lives. Similarly, at Phulaguri according to the inscription, out of 54 martyrs the names of only nine are available.

However, I think that the number of martyrs must surely have been even more than the estimates given in the inscriptions on the memorials, as so many deaths remained undocumented.

The list of all the memorials have been incomplete due to many reasons, a few being:

1. Official apathy to record the names of the martyrs in the

official documents.

2. To make the number seem lower than the actual for possible repercussion during that period.
3. Identification of dead bodies might have been a problem as people joined the meeting from far-flung areas.
4. Only names of the identified dead bodies found at the site of the incident were recorded.
5. Patharughat was not an easily accessible area in those days and therefore many names of the martyrs were missing,
6. Though Phulaguri was easily accessible, even then the names of the victims of the Phulaguri massacre were missing because it took place in 1861 when there was not much interest in peasant uprising as the politically conscious persons of Assam during that period were from the elite class.
7. The names of persons who succumbed to injuries from bullets and during the lathi charge later have never been recorded.
8. Even relatives of the martyrs never disclosed the names of the martyrs in fear of retaliation by the British administration.

Annexure II
Bhogeswari Phukanani

Bhogeswari Phukanani was born probably in 1885 at Barhampur of the Nagaon district of Assam. She was married to Bhogeswar Phukan and the couple was blessed with two daughters and six sons. She had been a very progressive lady much ahead of her time. She took active part in the Indian freedom struggle along with taking care of a large family. Despite being the mother of eight children, she not only led several non-violent freedom struggle activities, but also, unlike many leaders, she encouraged her children to join the independence movement of India. She always encouraged her children to lead the processions, unlike most of the leaders during that period of time.

Bhogeswari Phukanani was a very active Congress worker in the Berhampur, Babejia and Barpujia areas in the Nagaon district of Assam and became a thorn in the flesh for the British administration from 1921 onwards.

She was instrumental in setting up offices for the Indian National Congress in these areas. In 1930, Phukanani took part in the Civil Disobedience Movement under the leadership of Gandhiji. While as a mark of disobedience she joined a procession and also took part in picketing of government offices.

As a retaliatory move, the British administration arrested her in 1930 and put her behind bars for a few months. After her release from jail, she became more active and extremely vocal against the British administration. Her eloquence and organisational skills became a major headache for the district administration and she became a 'target leader'.

In 1942, the Indian National Congress office located at Barhampur was forcefully occupied by the British police and the office was closed for any activities pertaining to the freedom struggle by a specific order of the district administration to suppress the Quit India movement in that area. As expected, the Congress party organised a protest march against the high-handedness of the British authorities.

Phukanani with her sons took part in that protest march against the specific order which was nothing but the tip of an iceberg of a larger and ever increasing oppressive British policy in India. The protesters outnumbered the British police and were successful in reopening the Congress office by evicting the stooges of the British administration after they illegally occupied the same.

A celebration of their success was held on 18th September 1942 in the office premises or might be two days later on 20th September, 1942 as the documentation is not clear. Hearing about the massive gathering, the British administration sent a large police force to the Congress office forcefully to teach them a tough lesson. Many have claimed the British action was intended to destroy the office for good and break the moral of the local people who joined the Independence movement at the behest of the Congress leaders, including Bhogeswari Phukanani.

She sacrificed her life for our motherland when she was shot at by a captain of the British administration with his service revolver when Phukanani hit him with a pole of the tricolour. She fumed at the disrespect shown by the captain towards the flag and succumbed to her injuries and died on 20th September, 1942.

However, there are two versions regarding the way she attained her martyrdom. According to the first, Phukanani and a young lady named Ratnamala were leading a large group of people from the nearby villages with the flag in their hands. They were chanting 'Vande Mataram' and other popular slogans of the freedom struggle. The police party led by a captain tried to stop the procession and in the ensuing scuffle the British army captain grabbed the tricolour from Ratnamala, who fell to the ground. It is said, he tried to trample the flag to diminish the morale of the people in the procession.

Seeing the disrespect, Phukanani could not see any reason to control herself and she instinctively struck the captain on his head with the pole of her flag with all her might. However, being a lady about five feet four inches tall, she could not hit and injure the six-foot British officer with a helmet on his head. But her action infuriated the British officer as he perhaps thought it was a terrific blow on the British administration. He immediately pulled out his service revolver and shot the patriot point-blank.

According to the other version, Phukanani was not present when the British police, led by the captain, arrived at the spot. He ordered the crowd to demolish the Congress office by themselves. However, when she came to the office premises, she was furious to see a British official pointing a gun at her son and some of the others in the melee. She rushed to the captain and struck the official with the flag pole she was carrying. As he felt the blow was on British hegemony, as I've said earlier, the captain immediately shot at her point blank.

Again, there were two versions about her actual day of death. According to the first version, she had succumbed to the gun wound on the same day that Kanaklata also attained her martyrdom on 20th September 1942.

According to the second version, she had succumbed to her bullet injury three days after the incident that took place on 18th September 1942.

In any case, there was no dispute that she had also attained her martyrdom on 20th September, 1942 at the age of 57. Most historians mention her age as 45 when she attained martyrdom which does not seem to be true because her date of birth has been mentioned as 1885. Her date of birth and age at the time of martyrdom may be different from popular belief, but that does not lessen the love for her country and her bravery.

Her death and the circumstances leading to her death have been surrounded by a veil of mist, but her indomitable spirit and love for our motherland shines as brightly as the mid-day sun blazing.

After India gained its independence in 1947, the Nagaon civil hospital was renamed after her as was an indoor stadium at Guwahati. Many more memorials have also been erected in her memory.

ANNEXURE III
UNSUNG HEROINES AND LADY MARTYRS OF ASSAM TO BE REMEMBERED

In Assam, both men and women took active part in the freedom struggle and more than twenty percent of the martyrs from Assam were mothers and sisters. The following paragraphs are devoted to some female martyrs apart from Kanaklata Barua and Bhogeswari Phukanani.

Mungri alias Malati Mem, Lalmati, Darrang

She is one of the forgotten martyrs of Assam, perhaps due to her poor background or because she was not from the so-called mainstream Assamese society. She was from the tea garden community whose ancestors were brought to Assam from the Chota Nagpur belt (comprising parts of Orissa, Bengal, Jharkhand, Chhattisgarh and Madhya Pradesh) as cheap labourers by the British tea planters. They were brought and kept in inhuman conditions. Many perished while being transported and those alive were forced to stay and work without being provided any health care facilities. This resulted in large scale untimely deaths of these labourers. The use of opium was rampant among the hapless tea garden labourers. Mungri alias Malati Mem was leading an anti-opium campaign in the tea gardens of Darrang district. Her active participation in the anti-opium campaign made her the 'enemy number one' for the opium addicts and opium peddlers of these tea gardens. In 1921, she was murdered by drug-addicts at the behest of government officials at Lalmati in Darrang district for supporting Congress volunteers in their campaign for prohibition of opium. Many, however, claimed she was killed directly by British administration on some fictious grounds of treason against the British government. Though she is a revered person amongst the tea garden community, she is yet to get proper respect among the people of Assam, due to lack of publicity about her contribution to the country.

Dariki Dasi Baruah, Golaghat

She was a young lady who took active part in the Civil Disobedience movement in 1931 wholeheartedly. Again, she was involved in the anti-opium campaign launched by the congress party. She was arrested on 1st February, 1932 for picketing at government offices as part of the anti-opium campaign. After conducting a sham judicial procedure by the British administration, she was jailed for six months in Jorhat. She was pregnant at the time of her imprisonment. Though she was offered conditional release from jail, being a lady devoted to the country, she bluntly refused the offer. Eventually, she fell sick due to the unhygienic conditions of the jail. Due to lack of proper health facilities in the jail, she died on 26th April, 1932 during her confinement in Jorhat jail. She is yet to receive proper recognition as a martyr.

Rebati Lahon, Teok

She was an active participant and organiser of the Quit India movement in Teok at a very early age. She became an eyesore for the British administration for some time. A few days before the expected programme of flag hoisting on 20th September, she was picked from a meeting and put behind bars. She was kept in the Jorhat jail for the most part of 1942. During confinement in prison, she suffered from pneumonia. She was released from jail on the grounds of her poor health but succumbed to her ailment subsequently. She breathed her last soon after coming out of her imprisonment. She remains an unsung hero.

Khahuli Devi, Dhekiajuli

She was a newly married young lady from a very poor family. Though she was pregnant during that period, she chose to join the procession to the Dhekiajuli police station. She was shot by a policeman from point blank range without any physical threat from her. She died instantly and became another martyr in the Dhekiajuli on the 20th of September 1942, but remains unsung.

Tileswari Barua, Dhekiajuli

She took active part in the Quit India movement in and around Dhekiajuli Police station. In September, 1942, she was shot dead by the British police when she was trying to hoist the national flag at the top of Dhekiajuli police station removing the British flag indicating the end of the British Raj in India. Kanaklata Barua and she both attained martyrdom for our country, but she is also yet to get recognition from the people.

Kumali Devi, Dhekiajuli

She was the third brave heart who took British bullets to her chest at the Dhekiajuli police station on that fateful day, but remains largely unknown.

Padumi Gogoi, Dhekiajuli

She was a local Congress leader who had inspired many young people to join the Mrityu Bahini on 18th September, two days prior to the scheduled day of the flag hoisting programme at each and every police station of Assam to end British Rule in India symbolically. On the D-day, on 20th September, 1942, she was targeted by the police and was beaten mercilessly by lathis for a long time. When she almost lost conscious, she was arrested and sent to jail for six months. In the jail, as expected, she was not provided any treatment for her injuries. and she was physically and mentally devastated during her confinement inside the four walls of the prison. She had been physically and mentally broken. Her health deteriorated as her injuries remained untreated. She passed away a few days after her release from jail. Her supreme sacrifice for the country is also yet to receive recognition from the people.

Golapi Chutiani, Dhekiajuli

Her case was no different from Padumi Gogoi except that she was not arrested by the police after being grievously injured during the lathi charge by the British police. She was also wounded severely in the lathi attack and succumbed to her injuries within a few days of the deadly attack on 20th September, 1942. She was an unsung hero of Assam whom historians have ignored.

Thunuki Das, Dhekiajuli

She took part in the 1942 Quit India movement at Dhekiajuli as well. She was seriously injured in the lathi charge when the British administration let loose policemen with their lathis on the peaceful procession near Dhekiajuli police station on that fateful day. She succumbed to her injuries within a few days and till date her sacrifice and bravery have not been given their due.

Jaluki Kachariani, Dhekiajuli

She was a tribal lady of Dhekiajuli who participated in each and every programme of the Congress in its struggle to make India free from the British Raj. She was hit by a bullet in her stomach in the Dhekiajuli police firing on 20th September, 1942. Excessive bleeding and lack of medical treatment led to her death soon after the incident. She is yet to be declared a martyr.

Kon Chutiani, Dhekiajuli

She was another martyr of the dreaded lathi charge by the British police near the Dhekiajuli police station on 20th September,1942 who succumbed to her injuries a few days after the lathi charge. Her life also could have been saved, had she received proper medical care. She is yet to be declared a martyr and her supreme sacrifice remains unknown.

Lila Neogoni, Lakhimpur

She was the Lahkimpur version of Padumi Gogoi and Golapi Chutiani who had also been beaten up mercilessly by the British police of Lakhimpur police station while she was leading the procession to the Lakhimpur police station. She succumbed to her injuries two months later and remains an unsung hero.

The list of women martyrs is only exemplary, not an exhaustive one. There might be many more women of different ages who had laid down their lives during the freedom struggle of India about whom I, along with many, do not have any knowledge. I submit my unconditional apology to them and their family members for not writing anything about them. This always reminds me of the words on an epitaph in the War Memorial in Kohima:

Tell them when you return home, we laid down our lives for their better tomorrow.

The exact sentence though may be slightly different as I had seen it a few decades ago. I shall be very happy if a new generation of historians and research scholars are able to unearth the sacrifices of the unsung heroes and heroines of the India's freedom struggle spanning over more than a 150 years in India and 125 years in Assam, like present generation historians and research scholars in other parts of India are actively doing.

Annexure IV
Gentleman Martyr Kushal Konwar

Kushal Konwar was born on 21st March 1905 at Chaudang Chariali of Ghiladhari Mouza of present Golaghat district, a part of the erstwhile undivided Sibasagar district of Assam. He was the fifth child of his parents, Sonaram Konwar, and Kanakeswari Konwar. His family was one of the many branches of the Ahom royal family.

Kushal Konwar was a mild natured truthful child from his early age. He received his first schooling in the local Golaghat Bezbaruah School. He completed his primary school education in 1918 and got admission at the Bezbarua Middle English School at Golaghat. In 1921, even when he was in school, he was inspired by Gandhiji's call for non-cooperation and took an active part in it.

After completing his school education, inspired by the teachings of Gandhiji, Konwar established a primary school at Bengmai. Kushal Konwar married Prabhawati and the couple was blessed with two sons, Khagen Konwar and Nagen Konwar in due course of time. Later, according to some sources, he joined the Balijan Tea Estate as a clerk where he worked for some time before finally joining the independence movement as a full-time volunteer. He was instrumental in strengthening the Congress party in and around Sarupathar area. He led a group of youths to influence the locals to take part in the Satyagraha and Non-Cooperation movement against the British.

It has been claimed that from 1925 onwards, due to the influence of the ideals of Mahatma Gandhi, he changed his lifestyle completely. It is said Kushal Konwar became a vegetarian and carried the *Shrimad Bhagavat Gita* as his only companion whenever he was on tour. After the Salt Satyagraha led by Gandhiji in 1931, it is said that he had even stopped having salt till the last moments of his life.

As mentioned earlier, on 8th August 1942, the Congress Working Committee in its meeting in Bombay passed the Quit India resolution. Though Gandhiji appealed for peaceful non-cooperation and dharna, large scale violence took place in many places of the entire country. In many places, government offices were burnt down and in many places of India, government properties were damaged by the miscreants (a word widely used by agitators all over the world whenever the agitations go out of control of the leaders who officially propagate non-violent and peaceful protests). In some areas, road, rail, and telecommunication networks were disrupted by some antisocial elements (another word of convenience) taking advantage of the freedom struggle. During that period, Kushal Konwar was the president of the Sarupathar Congress Committee.

On the 10th of October, 1942, taking advantage of the thick fog in the early morning, some radical elements (a relatively honourable word used by historians for these groups of patriots) of the Indian struggle for independence removed some fishplates of the railway line near Sarupathar in Golaghat district. As expected by the militia, the passing by military train with over a thousand Allied soldiers derailed and as a result of that, many were killed and many more injured. The British police immediately swung into action by cordoning the entire adjoining area of the accident and searching for the alleged culprits. The district magistrate of Jorhat, C.A. Humphrey, issued arrest warrants for all the members of Indian National Congress of Sarupathar and its adjoining areas with immediate effect.

Being the president of the Indian Congress of the Sarupathar area, Kushal Konwar was accused of being the chief conspirator of the sabotage and was arrested by the police. It was ironical that one of the most ardent followers of Gandhiji and his principle of non-violence, Kushal Konwar was arrested for one of most violent incidents of Assam.

As he was completely ignorant about the sabotage plan and action thereon, he did not try to evade arrest by the British administration. He was picked up by the police from his residence. Subsequently, he was charged as the mastermind and was lodged in the Jorhat jail on the 5th of November 1942.

In another sham judicial mockery of pre-independence era, the court of C.M. Humphrey, Kushal Konwar was declared guilty without a single proof against him. He was sentenced to be hanged to death.

As a true follower of Bhagwan Shri Krishna, and as a learned man of the teachings of the holiest book of the Hindus, *Bhagavat Gita*, he accepted the verdict with all humility without showing any emotion except uttering a sentence with folded hands to the sky (ceiling of the room), “Oh, the Almighty, Owner of the Universe, I am thankful to you for choosing me to be an honoured martyr for my motherland.”

When his wife, Prabhavati visited him in the Jorhat jail, he repeated the same words to her by saying that he and his entire family should be grateful forever to the almighty as He had selected him to be one of the few his loved ones from among the lakhs of people for supreme sacrifice for the country. He further told her, thousands of people were made prisoners by the British administration for serving the country, but only a few got the opportunity to become martyrs. Therefore, instead of being unhappy, his family members should be proud as ‘members of the family of a martyr’. He told his wife Prabhavati not to behave as a hapless widow, but always lead life as the proud wife of Martyr Kushal Konwar. He promised to be present near her spiritually her entire life.

Kushal Konwar, unlike many of the prisoners, was always in a jovial mood and spent most of his time in confinement in prayers and reading the *Gita*. He did not show any sign of fear during the entire period in the death row cell of the Jorhat jail. The police records show that on 15th June, 1943 at 4:30 a.m. Kushal Konwar was hanged to death in Jorhat Jail.

Gandhiji spoke about his death: “He alone can be a true satyagrahi who knows the art of living and dying.”

Yes, Kushal Konwar lived with dignity, till the moment of his death, remaining a dignified man.

When Kushal Konwar became a martyr, both his sons were very young and they had to face a lot of financial problems. However, after independence, their welfare was looked after by the Government of Assam. They were able to settle quite comfortably in due course of time. His late elder son, Khagen Konwar was blessed with five sons and five daughters who may still be alive. The younger son, Nagen Konwar expired a few years ago, leaving behind two sons and his wife.

The people of Assam still remember the supreme sacrifice of Kushal Konwar and many institutions have been named or renamed after him.

According to British records, Kushal Konwar was involved in the violent incident, but according to the version of the Congress Party and common people of Assam, he was not involved. If, however, even if British version was truthful, we should be proud of Kushal Konwar, like we all Indians are of Martyr Bhagat Singh or Martyr Chandra Shekhar Azad. The only difference between Kushal Konwar and Bhagat Singh is that Kushal Konwar was one of Gandhiji's ardent followers and Bhagat Singh had never been glorified by the Congress party during their campaign against British rule.

ANNEXURE-V

Phulaguri Uprising of Assam

The agrarian Phulaguri Uprising (also known as Phulaguri Dhawa/Dhewa) was a proud and tragic chapter of the history of Assam. In October 1861, this farmers' protest took place at Phulaguri which is situated around 15 kilometres west of Nagaon town of Assam. It was launched against the new oppressive income and farm taxation policies of the British administration just after the first Indian Freedom struggle and popularly coined as the Sepoy Mutiny of 1957. Assistant Commissioner, Lieutenant B.H. Singer and two Indian police constables were murdered by unhappy peasants on 18th October 1861. A massacre that followed in the hands of British administration to crush the uprising led to unofficially 39 farmers being killed and hundreds injured. Unlike Champaran and some other peasant movements of mainland India, the glorious and tragic chapter of Phulaguri has been missing from the mainstream history of India.

After the Sepoy Mutiny, the Indian subcontinent became a dominion state of the British Empire. The British government asked the East India Company to bear the entire expenditure related to the suppression of the rebellion. The British Crown also wanted to recover the entire compensation amount to be paid to the shareholders of the East India Company after it took over all the assets and responsibilities of the subcontinent from the East India Company. The income and license taxes were imposed on Indian citizens to recover the said amount. The people of Assam also had to bear the brunt of the burden of heavy taxation by the British administration. In Assam, crops, fisheries, fodder, timber and trees on which silkworms were fed, had also come under the new taxation policy. A ban on poppy cultivation in 1860 reduced lives of many cultivators to penury. The East India Company had earlier encouraged poppy cultivation in India to export opium to China. However, after the Opium Wars ended with the Treaty of Tientsin, the British government who took over from the East India Company, had no more interest in increasing the production of poppy, as their market for opium had shrunk to a minimum level. The British government's decision to impose tax on betel leaf and areca nut farming was too much to digest for the farmers of Assam. In fact, imposition of tax on betel leaves and betel nuts by the British administration sparked the uprising of the farmers of Nagaon district at first.

A large group of farmers marched on 17th September, 1861 to submit a petition to the deputy commissioner of Nagaon, Lieutenant Herbert Sconce for the redressal of their tax grievances. The arrogant deputy commissioner refused to meet the agitated farmers. Infuriated by his refusal about eighteen farmers barged into his chamber, ignoring the objection raised by the sentries of the DC office. Then the police who were protecting the DC office, immediately arrested the farmers who forced their entry into his room.

The farmers again assembled in front of DC office to submit a memorandum on the 9th of October, 1861. Again, the arrogant DC refused to meet them but issued a statement that there was no plan to impose tax on betel farms.

After getting a second rebuttal from the British administration, the farmer leaders decided to convene a meeting of the farmers to take a decision on the future course of action. In that meeting, it was decided that whatever decision would be taken in the open meeting, would be binding for those who would be present in the meeting.

When Sconce was informed about the public meeting, underestimating the ground reality, he sent a small police force to arrest the organising leaders at Phulaguri. When a police force of five reached Phulaguri on the 15th of October 1861, they realised they were totally outnumbered by the agitating farmers. They appealed the crowd to disperse peacefully; expectedly, the farmers refused their appeal. The small police force had no alternative but to make a hasty retreat and informed their superior about the volatile situation at Phulaguri.

Deputy Commissioner Sconce sent reinforcements to the area with 13 additional policemen, including the Daroga (SHO) of Nagaon. The police party led by the Daroga, reached Phulaguri on the 16th of October, 1861; but they were horrified to see that there were at least three to four thousand farmers already present in the meeting, and the numbers were growing. Furthermore, a few hundreds were armed with lathis and other deadly weapons. After getting the information of the swelling number of agitators, Sconce sent another police force to assist the Daroga.

On 17th October 1861, again the police failed to persuade the organisers of the meeting to abandon the venue of the meeting peacefully. The police force tried to impress upon the farmers to end the meeting assuring the agitating farmers that they would arrange a meeting with the DC within a short time.

After having failed to convince the agitators to disperse, the Daroga reported back to the DC about his inability to convince the agitating farmers to disperse. After getting this information from the Daroga, Sconce sent Lieutenant G.B. Singer, Assistant Commissioner, with twenty more policemen.

Assistant Commissioner Lt. Singer reached Phulaguri on 18th October, 1861 and saw that the meeting of the farmers was going on in full swing. He told the spokesman of the farmers, Jati Kalita, that the meeting was illegal and that they should end it immediately. However, he assured the farmers that they could submit a petition to the authorities to consider their issues sympathetically. He ordered the policemen under his control to make the crowd disperse peacefully. Further, he ordered the policemen to disarm the armed farmers.

To encourage the policemen under his command, Singer snatched some lathis from the protestors by himself. However, when, Singer tried to disarm a farmer Moira Singh, a fisherman named Babu Dom, struck him on the head with a lathi. Then other farmers jumped upon the policemen without showing any mercy. Being totally outnumbered, the policemen fled from the scene leaving Singer alone to face the fury of the farmers. Singer was lynched and his dead body was thrown into the Kolong river by the agitating farmers. Thus, the first round's victory went to the farmers.

The DC, Sconce learnt about the killing of Assistant Commissioner, Lt. Singer and another policeman by the agitating farmers in the evening. Fearful of another attack by the agitating farmers, he sent half of his police force to Phulaguri to retrieve the dead body of Singer and the rest of the policemen were kept on high alert to guard the treasury. The police force was attacked by the farmers at Phulaguri on 19th October, 1861 for the second time.

Incidentally, and luckily for the British administration, Major Henry Hopkinson, the agent of the North East Frontier Governor General and Assam Commissioner, was on board a steamer near Tezpur. After getting the information of the uprising on 19th October, Hopkinson requisitioned the steamer and with the help of fellow-passenger, Major Campbell, he also requisitioned an armed force from the 2nd Assam Light Infantry and sent them immediately to Nagaon to assist the DC. Hopkinson himself went to Guwahati, took a battalion under Captain Chambers, and reached Nagaon on 23rd October 1861 to take control of the district.

The force of Campbell was also attacked by the Phulaguri farmers. However, on the 24th October, 1861, DC Sconce and Captain Campbell arrived at Phulaguri with a devious design to crush the agitation forever. This time, the farmers had to face the fire power of the British police. The lathi-wielding farmers were no match for the policemen with guns. In the ensuing battle on the banks of the Kolong river on that day, the brutal massacre of farmers took place. The British policemen unofficially killed 39 farmers and injured hundreds of farmers on that day. The incomplete list of martyrs is as follows:

1. Chuwabor Lalung
2. Thomba Lalung
3. Moira Singh
4. Leleu
5. Bhedeu
6. Nal Dom
7. Lahar Nath
8. Beer Singh
9. Hafiz Miya

The dead bodies were taken by the farmers to the bank of a *beel* (lake) five kilometres away from the place of firing at the middle of the night so that they could be consigned to flames keeping the dignity of the martyrs.

More than hundred farmers were arrested and imprisoned from Phulaguri and the neighbouring regions in a makeshift jail.

The armed forces were garrisoned at Phulaguri for the next six months. Further, to rub salt on the injury, the local farmers were forced to provide the best of the foods and comfortable accommodation to all the garrisoned armed forces for the entire period of their stay free of cost.

Lakshman Singh Deka, Sangbar Lalung and Rangbar Deka were hanged to death at Nowgong (present Nagaon) jail for killing Assistant Commissioner, Lt. Singer. Reportedly, no one was hanged for killing the Indian policemen.

Rupsing Lalung, Sibsing Lalung, Narsing Lalung, Hebera Lalung, Babu Dom Kaibarta and Banamali Kaibarta were given life imprisonment and deported for life to Kalapani in the Andamans by the Calcutta High Court.

Koti Lalung, Amba Lalung, Job Lalung, Katia Lalung, Mohi Koch, Kali Deka along with another 31 (names could not be retrieved) farmers were jailed in Calcutta for 10 years.

Two other accused (names could not be retrieved) were banished for 14 years and one was sent to jail to undergo rigorous imprisonment for seven years.

The local kings who suffered financially were five Tiwa kings – Ghana Sing (King of Tupakuchi), Subha Sing (King of Barpujia), Mothou (King of Khaigarh), the King of Sara Rajya, King of Mikir Rajya and seven kings of Mayang, Kumoi, Nellie, Baghara, Ghagua, Teetelia and Sukhanaguri.

Deputy Commissioner Sconce was also not spared by the British administration for his inept handing of the whole situation. He was demoted to the post of Assistant Commissioner and transferred to Kamrup district.

At present Phulaguri is a wealthy village with a good number of government officers and officials. The residents of Phulaguri are very proud of their ancestors for their bravery and patriotism.

(The accuracy of the dates cannot be ascertained as those have been taken from different sources.)

ANNEXURE-VI

Patharughat Uprising of Assam (1894)

Twenty-five years before the Jallianwala Bagh massacre, more than a hundred peasants fell to the bullets of the British police on 28th January, 1894, in Patharughat, a small village in Assam's Darrang district. Unfortunately, again this incident did not get any publicity in mainland India because of the apathy shown by the British historians as well as Indian historians carrying British legacy in their veins.

Patharughat Ran (Battle of Patharughat), like Kolongpar Ran at Phulaguri was also a fallout of the taxation policy of the British government. They were collecting tax in cash and sometimes the tax appeared to be as high as 80 percent of the income accrued from the agricultural land for which tax was imposed. As mentioned earlier many times, after the Yandaboo Treaty in 1826, Assam went to the East India Company. However, after taking over the Indian subcontinent as dominion state after the Sepoy Mutiny (touted as the first war of Indian Independence), the British administration conducted land survey to impose appropriate taxes on different agricultural products. Indian farmers were used to giving royal tax by giving a part of their agricultural products, and barter system was the main marketing system in pre-British era. But British completely changed the tax system by which Indian farmers were forced to sell their products in the market to pay taxes. That was the real problem faced by the farmers all over India. The farmers of Assam also faced the same problem and started showing their dissent by holding meetings and protests.

As the number of meetings and protests grew day by day, the British authorities declared that the peasant protests were unlawful and viewed them as grounds for treason against the country. However, that did not deter the farmers from holding meetings and protests against the taxation policy.

On the fateful day of 28th January, 1894, there was a huge gathering of farmers at a protest meeting at Patharughat (also known as Patharighat). The meeting was attended by farmers from Patharughat and its adjoining villages. As the meeting was in progress, on getting information of the meeting, Deputy Commissioner of Darrang district, J.D. Anderson, Superintendent of Police, Mr. Barrington and Sub-divisional Officer, Mr. Remington arrived at the venue accompanied by a battalion of armed police.

Instead of hearing the grievances of the farmers, the DC declared that under no circumstances the tax law would be repealed. The infuriated farmers repeated the same mistake of the farmers of Phulaguri about thirty-three years ago, tried to fight with their lathis against the policemen armed with guns. Unlike the Phulaguri farmers, the farmers of Patharughat could not gain even any initial advantage as the police force was large. To be fair to the farmers of Patharughat, it was a desperate attempt to show their angst against the unjust tax policy. However, the final outcome was one of the biggest tragedies in the history of Assam as more than a 140 farmers lost their lives in the police firing on that day itself. A good number of farmers succumbed to their injuries few days after the firing incident due to the lack of any medical treatment. Thousands were injured in the incident. However, the British official record showed only 15 casualties at Patharughat on that bloody day in Assam's history. By underreporting the casualties, the British administration tried to show the world that the Patharughat incident was a mere skirmish between police and a few farmers only, not a large-scale massacre.

However, the people of Assam will always remember the martyrs of Patharughat for their valour and supreme sacrifice for the farmers' cause. A good number of documentaries and few TV serials have already been made on the heroic people of Patharughat and its adjoining areas. However, unlike the Jallianwala Bagh massacre, the massacre of Patharughat is yet to be acknowledged at the national level.

Though the farmer agitation at Phulaguri and Patharughat were not part of the freedom struggle of India per se, these two agitations might have sowed the seeds of a longing for independence in the minds of common people. A longing to break free from the shackles of the British and inspiration to join the better organised freedom struggle against the British rule under the overall leadership of the Indian Congress. The entry of Mahatma Gandhi into the leadership of the Congress made all the difference in the freedom struggle of India in the eyes of common people of India. All the people, irrespective of caste and creed, jumped into the freedom struggle of India and turned it into a well-oiled mass movement.

The visits of Mahatma Gandhi to Assam since 1921 galvanised the Indian Independence movement in Assam and its adjoining states of the Northeast. And as a result of that development, majority of Assamese people extended their hands to the freedom struggle of India.

ANNEXURE- VII

Challenges and Contribution of the Tea Community in developing a Larger Assamese Community

Tea-garden communities are multi ethnic groups of tea garden workers. They consist of different ethnic groups, speaking different languages and dialects. These languages are mainly : Sora, Odia, Sadri, Kurmali, Santali, Kurukh, Kharia, Kui, Gondi, Mundari, etc. However, the Sadri language with some influence of local Assamese language became the lingua franca among these communities. Their ancestors were brought to Assam by the British tea companies as cheap tea garden labourers during mid-nineteenth century (1860-90s). They were transported from the backward regions of Jharkhand, Odisha, Chhattisgarh, West Bengal and undivided Andhra Pradesh.

The officially referred to 'tea-tribes' by the present Government of Assam are one of the most backward socio-economic communities of Assam. These heterogeneous, multi-ethnic people are found mainly in upper Assam, the Northern Bank of the Brahmaputra valley in lower and central Assam and Barak Valley where number of large tea gardens are situated. The estimated population of tea tribes in Assam may be around 6.5 million; out of which around 4 million are believed to be living inside the residential quarters of approximately a thousand large tea gardens, while the remaining 2.5 million are residing in the vicinity of these tea gardens as agricultural labourers and marginal farmers. Some are engaged in the forest sector also. A sizeable section of these communities, particularly those having Scheduled Tribe status in other states of India, and living mainly in the village areas other than tea gardens, prefer to call themselves 'Adivasis' and are known by the term 'Adivasis of Assam'.

When the ancestors of the present tea tribes were brought to the tea plantations of Assam over the years during British rule, they were denied all basic human rights. Due to unhygienic conditions in their transport system, many of the labourers perished on their way to their new home in Assam. Those who were able to survive the torturous journey, were put into ruthless conditions to extract maximum benefit from the tea plantation by the British management without showing any humanity or mercy towards them. After independence, the living conditions of those labourers working in the tea gardens have improved, but up to what extent is still debatable.

The British tea planters made overcrowded unhygienic barracks for the tea garden labourers, marking them as the 'Coolie line.' The word 'Coolie' had been used for the labourers by the tea garden authorities, and it had far-reaching consequences on the psyche of the local Assamese people as well as in the minds of these people. Now, this word cannot be used by law to demean them. Now, after Independence, there has been great improvement with regards to their living conditions through a number of legislations. However, it is felt, a lot more is desired to be done to improve the economic condition of the tea tribes of Assam.

In a recent major development, the central government led by NDA approved 'The Constitution (Scheduled Tribes) Order (Amendment) Bill 2019' in the Cabinet to accord 'Scheduled Tribe' status to at least 36 tribes of the tea tribe community. However, it is yet to be passed by the Parliament due to opposition by the communities that already have the ST status in Assam.

The issue of wage is another issue gripping the majority of this community in Assam. They are demanding an increase in the daily wages of the tea garden workers from the existing daily wage of Rs 167/- to Rs 350/- which is yet to be resolved.

The conflict and violence in the north-eastern part of India has not spared the tea tribes in the last few decades. They are also becoming the victims of a volatile social and political situation in Assam. There were two major ethnic clashes between Bodos and Adivasis during the 1990s. Hundreds of innocent people from both communities were the victims of the ethnic clashes; thousands being rendered homeless in the clashes of 1996 and 1998. However, most of the time both the communities live in harmony without any discrimination in the areas with intermarriage and collective participation in social functions being quite common.

The younger generations are better-educated and are becoming professionals in various fields, though there are not many highly trained professionals from these communities. Even in the recent 2011 census, the literacy level among the tea garden communities is below 50% against Assam's more than 70% overall literacy rate. The literacy rate among females is more dismal. Because of this, the girls of tea-garden communities are more vulnerable to sexual exploitation than the girls of other communities of Assam. Early marriages, if not child marriage per se, are prevalent.

Despite their backwardness, their variety and diversity in the cultural field have contributed to the development of Assamese culture over the last few decades. The major festivals celebrated by these communities are Fagua, Karam (festival), Jitia, Sohrai, Mage-Parab, Baha-parab, Tusu-Puja, Sarhul, Nowakhai, Lakhi-Puja, Manasa Puja, Durga puja, Diwali, Good Friday, Easter and Christmas. Through different folk music and dances, they showcase social issues, their lifestyles and their glorious history. *Dhols, manjiras, madars, kartals, tamaks, nagaras, nishans*, and *bansuris* are some of the musical instruments used by these communities. 'Jhumur' is the most famous folk-dance form among all the communities and now it is part and parcel of each and every cultural function of Assam. Another dance form, Karam dance is also an important dance form associated with the Karam festival. Other folk dance forms are Chhau dance, Sambalpuri Dalkhai dance, Santal dance, Kurukh dance and Kharia dance. These beautiful dances are performed by female dancers wearing their traditional red-bordered white saris while the male dancers don dhotis and kurtas with white turbans.

The economic contribution of the tea-garden communities towards the economy of Assam is most significant in terms of generation of female employment and generation of revenue for the state. It is worth mentioning here that Assam produces about 40% of India's total production of tea and India was producing more than 17% total tea production of the world in

2020. In other words, about 7% of the world's tea production came from Assam only. From the above statistics one can understand the economic contribution of these communities as we all know that tea industry is a labor-intensive industry and highly dependent on a large workforce.

With this background, let me jot down the contribution of these communities for our freedom struggle.

Though the tea garden communities remained oppressed primarily as plantation labourers, even then, during the pre-independence era they tried to protest against the atrocities of the British planters and managements many times. However, most of these protests were ruthlessly suppressed by the British managements. Unfortunately, most probably, the tea garden labourers did not get support or encouragement from most of the Indian National Congress leaders of Assam in those days. Most of the time, Indian Congress never tried to include the leaders of these communities in the policy making of the Congress to expand its bases to the people of these communities for their active participation in the Indian freedom struggle. Some leaders of these communities have alleged that in many cases, some of the Congress leaders even helped the British management to suppress the will of the labourers of the tea gardens for personal gains.

Though they were neglected by the Congress leadership for decades, many from the tea-garden communities actively participated in the Indian Independence movement. Some of the prominent people from these communities were, Gajaram Kurmi, Pratap Gond, Shamburam Gond, Mohanchal Gond, Jagamohan Gond, Bidesh Kamar Lohar, Ansa Bhuyan, Radhu Munda, Gobin Tanti, Ramsai Turi, Bishnu Suku Majhi, Bongai

Bauri and Durgi Bhumij who took active part in the freedom struggle of India.

While some of the martyrs of the freedom movement from Assam received the limelight, martyrs from these communities neither got the desired respect nor publicity from the historians of Assam and elsewhere. Nevertheless, the martyrs are still remembered by these communities and their contribution should not be ignored by any of us.

A few martyrs of these communities are Christison Munda, Doyal Das Panika, Mongol Kurku, Tehlu Saora and Bankuru Saora. Christison Munda who ignited a revolt across the tea gardens of Rangapara in 1915, was publicly hanged at Phulbari T.E (Rangapara) by the British administration after following a sham judicial procedure in 1916.

Malati Mem alias 'Mangri' Oraon of Tezpur Ghogara TE (near Tezpur) became the first ever woman martyr of Assam in 1921 who was killed by British police (or antisocials who were opium users or smugglers) while participating in the Non-cooperation movement.

The list of martyrs from these communities may be much longer than what I have procured.

Another incomplete list of freedom fighters from the chah mazdoor/ Adivasi community of Assam:

1. Motilal Bhumij
2. Jhagaru Gourh
3. Jaggarnath Bhuyan
4. Mohan Lohar
5. Sonu Digal
6. Mahabal Gourh
7. Pratap Gourh
8. Lalsai Gourh
9. Sambhu Gourh
10. Gadadhar Kurmi
11. Sambariya Nayak
12. Kandu Orang
13. Sampat Tanti
14. Baloram Tanti

15. Sonu Singh Ghatowar
16. Mari Prasad Gowala
17. Maha Singh Ghatowal
18. Arakshit Gannayak
19. Sukhlal Rajput
20. Prasanlal Ghatwal
21. Fagu Guwala
22. Bajiwa Kamar
23. Mahabir Bhakta
24. Biju Vaishnav
25. Aikan Vaishnav
26. Vaida Vaishnav
27. Nandsingh Ghatowar
28. Karma Gourh
29. Burkha Gourh
30. Babulal Karmakar
31. Hariram Khaira
32. Videshi Kamar
33. Raghu Kamar
34. Arti Kheria
35. Sanu Kheria
36. Mohan Muda
37. Atowa Muda
38. Ghotu Majhi
39. Brahma Modi
40. Radha Modi
41. Sutuwa Rajowar
42. Bunuk Rajowar
43. Ramdhar Rabidas
44. Gobin Chandra Tanti
45. Bharat Tanti
46. Dinbandhu Tanti
47. Ramsai Tanti
48. Samri Bhumij
49. Soma Bhumij
50. Lakshman Bedia
51. Arjun Ghatowar
52. Sunilal Ghatowal
53. Rupana Ghatowal
54. Mahi Prasad Gowala
55. Munsi Gourh
56. Hari Kurmi
57. Hemlal Kalandi
58. Mangal Kurmi
59. Sarman Kamar
60. Bagai Munda
61. Ranga Munda
62. Badi Munda
63. Naga Munda
64. Mohan Chandra Majhi
65. Mangra Orang
66. Samru Orang
67. Ganju Parja
68. Sahdev Panika
69. Videshi Pan Tanti
70. Dashrath Tanti
71. Hari Tanti
72. Banmali Tanti
73. Deoria Tanti
74. Lasika Telenga

75. Budu Oria
76. Mahabir Oria
77. Saraswati Oriyani
78. Bimla Oriani
79. Jingis Dusad
80. Sonaram Keot
81. Nabin Chandra Bhumij
82. Ramdhani Rajbhar
83. Kaliya Tanti
84. Gethuram Gourh
85. Nanku Ghatowal
86. Darath Gourh
87. Maliya Tanti
88. Raghuwa Tanti
89. Rubi Das Tanti
90. Jagbandhu Das
91. Dhukhiya Bhagat
92. Arjun Nayak
93. Jagmohan Gourh
94. Bagai Bawri
95. Ruplal Kurmi
96. Ansa Bhuyan
97. Radhu Muda
98. Jiban Lal Mahato
99. Baliya Bhuyan
100. Punu Orang
101. Ratiram Mahato
102. Birbal Kalindi
103. Manohar Kurmi
104. Koyla Majhi
105. Deen Ghatowal
106. Birua Rabidas
107. Nantu Gowala
108. Tikhu Das
109. Nand Sonar
110. Gurasan Kurmi
111. Pitambar Kurmi
112. Manai Sonar
113. Raghunandan Rabidas
114. Ramcharan Kurmi
115. Lakhan Nuniya
116. Baligobin Gourh
117. Garida Gowala
118. Lalu Karmakar
119. Khirdhar Bhuyan
120. Sukra Guwala
121. Mathura Rabidas

Under the leadership of these local leaders, tea communities had taken part in different programmes over the years announced by the national leadership of the Congress party. For that, many of them had to undergo inhuman torture at the hands of British tea garden management and British police from time to time. Like other leaders of the Congress party, these leaders also had to go underground for many years. Within the Congress, few top leaders were not only sympathetic to the tea community, but also encouraged few young leaders to join the Congress and fight for the country's freedom. These young leaders contributed immensely to the freedom struggle. After independence they joined hands with the national political parties, initially to the Congress party, to help in the development of their communities.

Considering their contributions on the socio-economic front and cultural front for so many years to the larger Assamese society, all of us should appreciate the contributions of the communities to the freedom struggle as well. The concerned authorities should try to solve the problems they are still facing because of the exploitation meted out against them over centuries by different exploiters in different forms and in different disguises.

Annexure VIII

Story of Mula Gabharu

Mula Gabharu was born in 1486 to the royal family of Susenphaa, the Ahom King from 1439-88, who was her great grandfather. Her grandfather, Suhenphaa (1488-93) also ruled the Ahom kingdom. Unfortunately, he was murdered treacherously in a palace coup. Her father, Supimphaa at a relatively young age of early forties became the king of the Ahom Kingdom (1493-97). Supimphaa also died in 1497 and Mula became fatherless. Her elder brother, Swargadeo Suhungmung Dihingia Raja succeeded his father Supimphaa at the young age of twenty-five, but with an extremely matured head as the new king of the Ahom kingdom. Luckily for Mula, her elder brother was a wonderful brother who became a father figure to Mula and the other younger siblings from his own mother and stepmothers. Mula was different from the other girls in the royal family. She loved the *hengdan* (heavy sword used by the Ahoms in the wars/ battles) more than crockery and cooking. She liked to spend more time in the *yudha krira bhawan* (*akhara* in North India or the practice hall for the warriors) than in the kitchen. Eventually, in the akhara, she met her love in Frasengmung, the second son of the Borgohains of the Ahom kingdom. Her love story with the weapons and her future husband Frasengmung became a folklore for generation after generation.

As Mula grew older, Swargadeo Suhungmung Dihingia Raja personally taught his sister the nitty-gritty of horse-riding and the best use of weapons. Within a few months of training, she became an excellent cavalry to the delight of her king-brother.

"Can I lead an army in war one day?"

"You are capable of doing that. But I hope that day will not come during my regime when my sister has to face an army in the battlefield."

"Why do you think so, *kakaideo* (dear elder brother)?"

"Normally we never allow our sisters, daughters and wives to go to the battlefield. All men promise their sisters, daughters and wives to protect them till they are alive. It is only in our absence that you will have to protect yourselves. Therefore, my little sister, never ever dream of leading an Ahom army in the battlefield."

"Okay, Kakaideo, I shall never wish to lead an army in the battlefield. But if unfortunately, it is forced upon me by some compelling situation, I promise you, I shall do something special for which you, your children and my children will never be ashamed of me," she said hugging her beloved brother.

From the early years, she was made to understand that country and subjects are above the king, and the protection of the boundary and lives of the citizens are the most important duties of a king.

Swargadeo Suhungmung Dihingia Raja started considering Mula as a different kind of young lady after knowing about his sister's extraordinary love for her country.

Many people may question the decision of the king a few decades later, allowing his sister to move to the warfront when her husband lost his life fighting with the invaders led by Gaur commander, Turbak Khan. Against the same adversary, he himself almost lost his eldest son, Suklen who was critically injured and also lost the battle. Ton Kham, son of Mula Gabharu was also about to fight along with his maternal uncle, Kancheng Borpatra Gohain (stepbrother of the King and Mula) even after the death of his father. Then why did he allow his sister to fight against Turbak Khan?

Yes, he had let his sister to go to the battle field mainly for two reasons: he knew very well that without Frasengmung, she would not live long. Dying in the battlefield like a true warrior, had been a better proposition than dying as a hapless widow. The second reason was more intriguing than the first one. As siblings, when they played as aggressor and defender, Mula always played the role of a defender. She reminded her elder brother about her childhood dream of defending the borders of their motherland. She only asked her brother one thing, "Oh my brother, the king of Ahom kingdom, my son lost his father at an early age. But still, he is young and needs guidance. You have always played the role of my father. Therefore, please love my child as a father of your beloved Borgohain Frasengmung and also love him as a grandfather of your elder daughter, Mula."

Embracing his most loved sister, the king declared, "I do not know what is in store in the future, but so long I shall be alive, I shall treat Ton Kham as my own son."

Mula wiping her tears, said goodbye to her elder brother and proceeded to the battle field few hundred kilometres away.

Two decades after her completion of her training in the use of weaponry while riding on a horse. In 1532, she fought against the aggressive invaders under the leadership of Turbak Khan. Though she could not kill Turbak Khan by herself nor see his beheading by her younger brother, the Ahom soldiers were encouraged to see few Ahom women cavalry alongwith thousands of ordinary women in the battle field led by Mula Gabharu and conquered the enemy and snatched the victory for the Ahoms from the jaws of defeat. In that battle, women warriors Jayanti, Pamila, Lalita and some others on horseback were the companions of Mula Gabharu from the capital, who also sacrificed their lives for the country. According to some historical accounts, 50 widows of the aristocrats of Ahom Kingdom joined Mula Gabharu in her epic battle of Dikarai to take revenge of killing of their husbands. However, Mula was also joined by many widows of lower-level soldiers who were not trained warriors but full of patriotism and bravery. Some males who were common people of the countryside also joined Mula Gabharu in her fight of revenge and sacrifice. Those widows and common men were carrying machetes and spears used for killing wild animals to fight against the invaders. Though many of the widows and all the women cavalry were killed by the trained Army of Turbak, their sacrifices were written in golden letters in Assamese history for their valour, love for the country and love for their husbands. On that day, Assamese ladies became free of any purda system which prevents ladies of many parts of India to progress shoulder to shoulder in any fields, including the battle fields. That was the beginning of a new era of the Assam History.

Coming to her early life once again, when Mula was a seventeen-year-old, her trainer told her that she had to face the second son of the Borgohain of the Ahom Kingdom, a young man in his early twenties in a duel.

"Why should I face a male in a duel? Why I am not pitted against a female warrior?" Mula innocently asked her trainer.

"My child, for a friendly competition, a girl is pitted against a girl. But in a real battlefield, you may have to face an even more powerful male. In that case, you have no choice but to fight with the leader of the enemies. Frasengmung is reasonably good in use of all weapons. But I have found him excellent in strategy formulations which are more important in a war than just a skilful warrior or a mere strong warrior. Mula, always remember, a duel is won by a person who is physically strong, intelligent and knows the use of weapons extremely well. On the other hand, a battle can also be won by a leader who can lead his team from the front, but a war can be won only by a master strategist from behind or in a board room. He or she may be far away from the war zone, but can see the strategy of his opponent much before the enemies execute their plans. A duel lasts for few minutes or may linger for hours at best; a battle lasts for few hours to a day. But a war can range for few days to few months or even for years. Therefore, a country needs a person with matured head who never loses his patience and can convince the king to continue the war even at the loss of few reversals in some battles which may be parts of a long-drawn war. At present, I see a lot of potential; rather maximum potential in this young man. His extraordinary quality of coolness and farsightedness is the mainstay of this young man. He has a matured brain of a fifty-year war veteran. If he stays loyal to the king and the king utilises his capability in the proper way, our king will never taste any defeat in any war in his lifetime." The trainer stopped there but his introduction about the young man ignited the heart of Mula into a fire of love which did not diminish till her death almost three decades from that day.

At that moment Mula's sixth sense told her that she was not going to meet a person who would be fighting with her in a duel; but the person would be very special to her. Her inner voice all of a sudden told her, "You are going to meet your future husband." She was surprised that her heart started thumping like never before.

After a few minutes, Mula saw a tall slim young man entering the training hall. The trainer whispered something in his ears. He nodded with a smile and came towards Mula.

Mula was a tall, slim girl, but when Frasengmung came up to her, she had to look up to see Frasengmung's eyes. He was at least six inches taller than Mula. Their eyes met and the inevitable chemistry developed immediately. It was love at first sight. Both of them wanted to embrace tightly so that there should not be any space between their bodies for even a needle. But they could not do that because many pairs of eyes were on them witnessing the meeting of two legends.

"Are you ready, Mula, to fight with me?" Frasengmung asked Mula with a smile.

"No. I shall not be able to fight with you my entire life," Mula told Frasengmung as if she was talking in a dream.

"Why?"

"I do not know. However, to honour the order of my teacher, I shall engage myself in a mock fight with you."

"Of course, it will be a mock fight only. I also cannot hurt you. After all, you are a princess and younger sister of the King," Frasengmung told her with a teasing voice.

His teasing tone could not penetrate her brain. "How should I address you? I mean should I address you as sir?" Mula asked Frasengmung innocently.

"No!"

He told her softly, *"Bangahardeo."* (The word Ahom ladies, particularly the royals and aristocrats use to address their husbands.)

Mula flushed. Frasengmung thought he had crossed the line. "I am sorry, Mula. I should not have said that."

"Why? Now you have to allow me to address you like that only," Mula told him with a smile.

Pleasantly surprised, Frasengmung wanted to give a fitting reply to her tacit admission of her love for him; but the trainer called out, "Ok, you must have introduced yourselves by now. Now, it is time for the duel."

Mula attacked Frasengmung with different blunt weapons. Frasengmung did not engage in any counter attack. Then Frasengmung attacked Mula with different weapons, Mula defended. Frasengmung realised that Mula was really good at using different weapons. Though Frasengmung could have won very easily, he allowed Mula to win the duel as well as his heart.

Praising her skills, and taking permission from the trainer, Frasengmung left the training hall along with Mula's heart.

The trainer who was Frasengmung's maternal uncle whispered in his ears before the duel, "Do not sway with the will to win the duel. Always remember, you always have to protect her, not to hurt her. I saw a legend in her from the very first day."

But Frasengmung did beyond the advice of his uncle; he won the heart of the princess but lost his own to her as well.

That evening when Mula met her King-brother, she declared jubilantly, 'Kakaideo, today I did something to make you proud of your sister.'

"I am always proud of you Mula. Now tell me what you have done today?"

"I defeated Frasengmung Borgohain, the second son of your Borgohain in a duel." Mula was still in seventh heaven as she thought she had done something exceptional.

"But that is very old news for me. Narottam (the trainer) asked my permission in the morning itself to arrange a duel with Frasengmung to test your mettle." The cool response from her brother king made her a little bit upset.

"What happened?" Suhungmung became anxious at seeing the unhappy face of his sister.

"Perhaps you did not understand properly. I defeated Frasengmung in a duel today," Mula emphasised.

The King laughed for a while and called his sister near him.

"My child, Frasengmung was employed by his uncle, Narottam to test your capability as a warrior; not to have a duel with you. You fought for a win; but he tested your level of capability in the use of weapons. I saw his capability as a warrior when he defeated ten war veterans in his passing out parade along with some other trainees from the royal academy. Anyway, I am happy that you have passed your test as a good warrior. Narottam told me that you fought well with Frasengmung."

Mula flushed with shyness for her stupidity but with an unknown happiness at her brother's praise of the test of capability in the use of weaponry.

Fast-forward to the time after many years of their marriage. Her husband had gone to battle against Turbak, an invader sent by the Sultan of Bengal in 1532. After seven days since Frasengmung had left his home, the news of the death of her husband came as a bolt from the blue. As Ton Kham, their eldest son was on the way to the battlefield, all the last rites were done by Mula's second son Mon Kham.

Frasengmung Borgohain's rituals were completed on the second day after getting the news of his death by the King and Mula Gabharu.

Mula Gabharu blamed herself for the unfortunate and unexpected turn of events, as she could not give a '*kavash kapor*' to protect her husband in battle as she was on her periods prior to the day of leaving to the battlefield by her husband. Kavash kapor was a piece of protective cloth which had to be woven the previous night by the wife of the warrior if the warrior was a married person. If, however, he was not married, the protective cloth could be woven by his mother or sister.)

For a few hours she cried for her brave husband. But after that, she took the most unexpected and unheard decision for a royal lady of the Ahom kingdom; she would go to the battlefield to fight with the Mughals. During the mourning period, she promised to avenge her husband and the freedom fighters of the Ahom kingdom. After that, on the third day, she took a hengdan and went to her brother and King of the Ahom kingdom to take his permission to join the war.

"Kakaideo, my husband sacrificed his life for the motherland. I have to complete his incomplete work of driving out the invaders from the boundary of our motherland. Now, it is your duty to send your sister to the battle field to fight against the invader, Turbak Khan. If I win, that is very good; but if I lose my life while fighting, you will be remembered for your sacrifice of your sister for the motherland. I am going alone to the battlefield and challenge a duel with Turbak Khan."

Initially, Swargadeo Suhungmung Dihingia Raja tried to dissuade Mula, but finally gave his permission with a heavy heart and said, "I do not know, whether history will glorify me for my sacrifice as a brother or not; but definitely I shall be remembered as a king who could not stop his sister from going to the battlefield to defend the boundary of the motherland."

Then he hugged her beloved sister with a brooding feeling that it was their last hug.

She being a trained warrior decided to join the Ahom army alone in the battlefield. But her decision encouraged other widows who were also professionally trained warriors to join their leader, Mula Gabharu, the evergreen and energetic wife of the deceased Borgohain.

The next morning, she was accompanied by another forty-nine women on their horses from Garhgaon who were also trained warriors and lost their husbands in the war against the Mughals. On their way, many women who were not even trained joined the brigade with machetes in their hands. On the way some untrained men also joined their counterparts. In other words, if a woman joined Mula and her 49 cavalries in her journey to the battlefield, either her husband or her son or both had also joined Mula's brigade with some sort of weapons in their hands. Those weapons included types of swords to even whole bamboos with sharp edges. It is said that even a few Brahmins and Mahantas joined Mula Gabharu with small sticks in their hands; sticks which were used to control pets in their home. Such was the response of the common people to join the brigade of the Assamese army led by princess Mula Gabharu on that day. None imagined on that day that they were going to be a part of the history of Assam written in golden letters for generations to come.

Mula formed an army of her own with common people who were mostly untrained in warfare. The army led by Mula was large but lacked discipline, training and experience of any battle. However, they were determined to throw out the Bangals. As they did not have a plan and strategy, they were not sure where the army led by Konseng and Ton Kham were located. As a result of that, Mula and her army of common people reached the battle field without meeting the elite force led by her brother, Konseng Barpatra Gohain and her son, Ton Kham.

Just before entering the battlefield, she addressed the accompanying common people who were not experts in using any types of weaponry in a battle.

"I know you are not experts in using weapons normally used in a battle. But you are experts in killing mad dogs on the street. The soldiers led by Turbak Khan are nothing but a bunch of mad dogs and therefore they are to be killed by clobbering; we all are experts at that. We all are wearing very strong armours – that is love for our motherland and our patriotism. We can be killed, but never be defeated. So, raise your arms for the final sacrifice for our motherland. Now listen to me carefully, we shall use our strong ropes to control the cavalry's speed by entangling the ropes in between the legs of the horses. If we are lucky, some of the horsemen will fall from the horses. In that case I need not have to tell you how you should kill them without showing any mercy. I request those friends of mine who can throw fish nets properly, to try to put fish nets on the heads of the cavalry and foot soldiers. If you are successful, rest of our brothers and sisters will clobber them to death. Use your whole bamboo such a way that your enemy cannot come near to you. We shall try to snatch their weapons and use those against them. If any foot soldier surrenders, disarm them, tie their hands but do not kill them because they are also from poor families like many of us. But do not show any mercy on their leaders and cavalry men. They are from rich families; they came here to rule us. If they have skills, we have numbers. If they kill one of us, we shall pounce upon him so that his skill will be useless before our people. Remember if we die, we shall be welcomed in heaven not only by the gods, but also by our ancestors. Remember at any time, you have to try to kill at least one, before you are killed by them. Now, take the name of our God and cheer with me, *"Jai Ai Matri, tarile desh, marile swarga!"* (Hail our motherland, who defends motherland, if he dies, he/ she surely will get a seat in the heaven).

Everyone in the crowd shouted back, *"Jai Ai Matri, tarile desh, marile swarga! We shall drive away the invaders."*

When they arrived at the battlefield, it was already around eleven in the morning. Turbak and his army were not aware of the unexpected attack as they had information that the regular army of Ahom kingdom were in their camps almost twenty kilometres away from Dikarai Bank. The sentinels of Turbak's army saw swarms of people coming from the eastern sides of their camps. They also understood from the body language of the swarms of people that those people were not friendly as they were shouting, "Kill the Bangals! Drive away the Bangals!"

Accordingly, the sentry informed their bosses and the super boss, Turbak Khan about the arrival of thousands, if not lakhs, of unfriendly people in the vicinity of the Dikarai Bank. As the Turbak army were trained and ready for any such attack at any time, they immediately took their positions to defend themselves and carry out a counter attack on the crowd.

However, as they saw the people coming to attack were common people led by a lady, they started laughing among themselves and only a handful of cavalry were sent by Turbak Khan to stop the people. Underestimating the morale of the people and their leader, that morning at Dikarai, the Mughal army mocked the Ahom army saying that the Ahoms were so scared to face the Mughals that they had to send women and peasants to the war field. Mughal Army grossly underestimated the might of Assamese common people under the leadership of Mula Gabharu. Before they could realise the skills of the Assamese lady warriors in warfare, they lost few of their cavalries and hundreds of foot soldiers at the hands of fifty odd lady cavalries and thousands of foot soldiers of Assam. Many of the cavalry were clobbered to death as the number of common people was much more than the army of Turbak Khan.

Turbak Khan soon understood the gravity of the situation and ordered for an all-out counter attack on Mula's untrained armies. Even with all his might he and his cavalry could not move as fast as he wanted as his army was outnumbered by the ordinary people of Assam. But even then, he could see the dazzling beauty on the rampage and wondered who she might be!

He asked one of the bodyguards the identity of the rampaging beauty. Within a minute, Turbak Khan was told by the guard, "She is the wife of Frasengmung Borgohain and younger sister of the king."

Turbak Khan with a devious smile told his guard, "Do not kill this beauty. I need her for myself."

His message was conveyed to his soldiers and that was the gravest mistake Turbak Khan had committed in his entire life. In the attempt of arresting Mula Gabharu who was surrounded by her soldiers, the common people, Turbak Khan lost many cavalries either to the Ahom women warriors or at the hands of the common people. From a distance when Turbak Khan saw how his cavalries were losing their heads, his desire to enjoy his night with Mula evaporated like camphor in open air. He galloped towards Mula with a desire to kill her, not to arrest her.

When she saw for the first time her husband's murderer, Commander Turbak Khan in the war zone, her blood started boiling. She shouted at Turbak Khan like a wounded tigress, "I am Mula, widow of Frasengmung. Today no one can save you from my hengdan. I challenge you; if you are really a brave man, fight with me. Do not send your archer to kill me from a hiding place, from a safe distance like a coward!" Saying these words, she headed towards the Mughal commander like a Royal Bengal tigress.

As she proceeded towards Turbak Khan, few Mughal cavalry came to stop her progress towards their General. Turbak Khan told them to allow her to fight with him to satisfy her ego before her death.

As they started fighting, Turbak understood, he was lucky that someone else had killed Frasengmung treacherously and he did not have to fight with Frasengmung hand to hand. (According to me, Frasengmung was not killed by Turbak Khan in a duel, but was killed by an Assamese soldier to take revenge for annexing Chutiya Kingdom a few years ago.) As the duel proceeded, Turbak praised without uttering a single word that Mula Gabharu was not an ordinary woman, as he had thought, only an hour ago. But slowly, Mula became exhausted due to her long tiring travel before reaching the battlefield along with her drained energy due to her sorrow of losing her husband. For a moment she lost her concentration and that was enough time for the long spear of Turbak to pierce her bosom.

She fell from the horseback and tried to pull out the spear instinctively. Turbak Khan came down from his horse and told Mula Gabharu, "I never thought an Ahom Royal lady is so strong and an expert in the use of arms. I salute you for your bravery and expertise in weaponry. As you are leaving this world, let me tell you the truth surrounding the death of your husband. Your husband was not killed by an arrow of our archers. He was killed by an arrow of your own man from a blank range and that is why he was killed instantly. No arrow from a distance of a hundred odd metres could have killed your husband. I think the same arrow from a betrayer of your army will finish the Ahom kingdom in near future. Now no one can save your king from me."

Pulling all her energy to her voice she said, "I thank you for telling me the truth that you were not able to kill my husband in a duel. He was a tiger. But remember, he was an old tiger; he left two more young tigers as his sons and two adult tigers in two of my brothers. One is enough to kill you in the next battle to take revenge of killing the original tiger by deceit and killing of their widowed mother or sister. So do not be happy at my death; your days are already numbered." Saying all these words, she closed her eyes forever.

Hearing those words from dying Mula Gabharu, Turbak Khan started feeling a kind of loneliness amidst his waning Army. He looked around; in any of the battles he had fought so far when he was able to kill the leaders, all their soldiers used to run for their lives. But on that day, he saw something different: the common people did not leave the battleground after the death of their leader; rather they were shouting, "Our mothers, Mula and her companions have sacrificed their lives after killing hundreds of Bangals, now it is our turn either to kill them or to die for the motherland. So, chase the Bangals and kill them. Otherwise, our ancestors will disown us as their descendants being traitors who cannot defend their mothers and sisters!"

At their war-cry, a fear of death had taken over the mind of Turbak Khan. He felt his spirit to fight with the Assamese army sinking. He wanted to run away from the battle field to save his life. His mind was frozen with an unknown fear.

Finally, Mula Gabharu lost her life along with her ferocious battalion of fifty odd lady cavalries and hundreds of ordinary but extremely brave foot soldiers of adjoining areas of Dikarai at the hands of Mughal cavalries. As the sun was shining on their heads bestowing the blessings of immortality to the brave common people of Assam and fifty women warriors of Assam, Mula Gabharu's name had been written with golden letters in the annals of history as the bravest of all. She became the epitome of courage, sacrifice and patriotism for the generations to come.

However, unfortunately, the news of his mother's participation in the battle reached her son and brother only after an hour when they were discussing their plan to attack the enemy army led by Turbak Khan.

On the way to the battlefield, Ton Kham and Konseng came to know that Frasengmung had made the supreme sacrifice for the motherland. Instead of crying, Ton Kham told to his uncle, "I am lucky to be the eldest son of a great warrior, master strategist and above all, a great patriot. He has given me an opportunity to prove myself that I am at least equally good in warfare and a person of the highest degree of integrity. I shall be remembered as I am the eldest son of a great martyr."

"Yes, Ton, I am proud of him as a junior associate working with him for a decade or so. We have to plan meticulously to defeat the Bangals and sever the head of Turbak Khan from his body. We should not be in a hurry to jump into the battle without a proper plan and for execution of our plan, we must take immediate action to boost the sagging morale of the soldiers. After the martyrdom of Borgohain, their moral must have been very low as they even in their wildest imagination could not have thought that Frasengmung Borgohain can be killed by an enemy arrow," Konseng was calm as usual.

'Yes, *Mama* (younger brother of his mother), I fully support your plan to wait for an opportune time to attack on the Bangals."

As they were planning an attack on the army of Turbak Khan, a spy from the war zone informed Konseng about Mula Gabharu's attack on Turbak's army. Konseng told his nephew, "This is the opportune time to motivate our brave soldiers to attack Turbak Khan's army."

He called all the soldiers and addressed them with his hengdan pointing towards the sky, "My extremely brave and beloved soldiers, god and our ancestors are looking at us. They want that we should drive our enemies out of our boundary. My elder sister, Mula Gabharu, wife of our great general, Frasengmung Borgohain and the common people are fighting for our motherland. We cannot wait for even a single minute in the camp. Let us go and drive away the Bangals from Assam."

This was all that the soldiers needed to hear and they were energised for the fight of their life.

They reached the battlefield within one hour of hearing the news. But they were a little late. By then, Mula became the second martyr from the same family within a span of seven days. As Turbak Khan rode on his horse, he was challenged by Konseng for a duel.

Turbak saw his death in the 'Naga jathi' (long handled spear used by Naga people in the hunting of wild animals and in a battle) of Konseng. Already exhausted from his fight with Mula for the past hour, Turbak wanted to avoid a fight with the young general. He looked for his body guards; but he saw the nearest body guard was at least ten metres away from him, fighting with few common lathi wielding people.

To recoup his strength Turbak told Konseng, "I have killed Frasengmung and then his wife, Mula and if you fight with me, I have to kill three persons of the same family. So, if you want to live for a few days more, go away from my sight."

He knew that Konseng would not go away; but he wanted some time to rest his exhausted shoulders.

But Konseng was in no mood to talk with the murderer of his sister and brother-in-law. The very news of the death of his sister made Konseng so angry that without uttering a single word, he attacked Turbak. Turbak Khan realised Ahom generals were different from those in other places of India where they wanted to show their greatness by talking grandly, and even in some cases, letting the enemies escape from their clutches just to show how brave and powerful they had been.

Turbak Khan's right hand was severed by Konseng's hengdan. He looked for some help from his bodyguards by shouting,

"Where are you bastards? You are paid to save my life from the enemies, not to run away from the battlefield!"

But his shout drowned in the shouts of the common people, "Oh Great General, Konseng, kill him! Do not show any mercy to the sinner who killed your sister a few minutes ago!"

Konseng did not show any mercy on Turbak Khan and with another heavy blow of his hengdan, he chopped off his head.

As his head hit the ground, the Mughal army started fleeing from the battle field. Many of the Mughal soldiers were captured and some of them were killed in the next few hours, and all the firearms were confiscated.

By that afternoon, Konseng retrieved the body of his sister, Mula Gabharu, the fearless woman warrior of Assam with a heavy heart, but with a feeling of pride of being her younger brother.

Konseng took possession of the body of his sister and then took the severed head of Turbak in a shawl to hand over to his elder brother, Swargadeo Suhungmung. However, in the meantime, Swargadeo also arrived at Kaliabor to know the result of the battle. In fact, he became restless after sending his most beloved sister Mula to the battle field against his will.

After killing the Mughal invader, Konseng Borpatra Gohain called his nephew close to him and said, "I know you are very sad to lose your parents. I am also very sad to lose my elder sister and my most respected brother-in-law in this battle. But we are soldiers; we do not have time to mourn. Therefore, oh my dear son, pursue the Mughals up to Kortowa river (of present North Bengal) and put up a *choki* for us (for the Ahom Kingdom). Do not pursue them beyond Kortowa, because we are not greedy to take others' land; that was the boundary of the King of Kamrup. Chutiyas are descendant of the King Narakasura, the King of Kamrup. After taking possession of the Chutiyas' heirlooms our Swargadeo is the legitimate ruler of the Chutiyas and by virtue of that the entire kingdom of Kamrup is our territory."

"Do not worry, Mama, I shall do that gladly. My father taught me that a successful person never cries, because he has no time for crying. I know if I have to be successful in my life, I have to forgo my personal emotions to serve the country in a better way," Ton Kham replied with a sad smile.

Ton Kham pursued the Mughals up to Kortowa and established an Ahom post overlooking its boundary for almost another hundred years. According to some chronicles, Gaur

Nawab sent a daughter to Ahom harem as a token of goodwill for the Ahom king through Ton Kham. Incidentally, this was the furthermost Ahom post constructed by any general of the Ahom kingdom. Even the state boundary of modern Assam is inside this boundary.

After one month, when Ton Kham reached Gargaon, the capital of Ahom Kingdom, as per the rituals, his maternal uncle, Swargadeo Dihingia Raja took him on his lap as his own son and declared him as the new Borgohain of his kingdom. Thus, the baton of Borgohain had been passed on from father to his son in a sombre function. Ton Kham had to take over the post of Borgohain without the presence of his parents. However, in my opinion, both Mula Gabharu and Frasengmung Borgohain were not only present on that occasion spiritually, but they were and are also still present when a brave son or a daughter of India becomes a martyr irrespective of caste, creed and religion.

I am sure on 20th September, 1942 as well, Mula Gabharu was spiritually present at the site where Kanaklata Barua was consigned to flames in the presence of thousands of mourners in Barangabari and its adjoining areas.

Bibliography

1. *Asomor Mahiyashi Nari* by Smti. Lokeswari Handique.
2. *Jyoti Prapat* by Smti. Lokeswari Handique.
3. The translated version of the original novel, *Mrityu Vijayani Kanaklata,* written by Dr. Biren Barkotoky and translated by Shri Deviprasad Bagdodiya.
4. A number of articles on Kanaklata Barua written by Smti. Lokeswari Handique.
5. A number of articles on Kanaklata Barua written by Shri Nagen Konwar.
6. *Bharatar Swadhinata Andolanat Asomor Chah Gosthi/ Adivasir Avadan* by Shri Nakul Kurmi